Combating
Managerial Obsolescence

Combating Managerial Obsolescence

Andrew N. Jones

Cary L. Cooper

PHILIP ALLAN

Distributed in the United States by

Greenwood Press
88 Post Road West
Westport, Connecticut 06881

First published 1980 by
PHILIP ALLAN PUBLISHERS LIMITED
MARKET PLACE
DEDDINGTON
OXFORD OX5 4SE

0 86003 509 3

British Library Cataloguing in Publication Data

Jones, Andrew Noel
    Combating managerial obsolescence.
    1. Executives, Training of
    I. Cooper, Cary Lynn
    658.4'07'124   HF5549.5.T7

ISBN 0-86003-509-3

Set by MHL Typesetting Limited, Coventry
Printed in Great Britain at
The Camelot Press Limited, Southampton

To Marie, Karl, Tara and Ciara for their
support and tolerance

To June, Scott and Beth for their
forebearance

To Dolores and Pat for their secretarial
help

The study on which this book is largely based
and which is referred to repeatedly throughout
the book as that of the book's authors was in
fact carried out by the Research and Planning
Division of AnCO — the Irish Industrial Training
Authority under the leadership and direction of
Dr A.P. O'Reilly.

The study was carried out by AnCO with the
support of the EEC Commission's Directorate
General for Social Affairs with whose permission
the results were published by AnCO under the
title of 'Keeping up-to-date as a Manager; a study
of occupational obsolescence among Managers
in Ireland'.

The copyright of such published work which
includes the questionnaire used in the study (a
copy of the questionnaire appears in Appendix
1 of this book) is the property of AnCO.

Constant change
is here to stay

Contents

List of
Figures and Tables

Figures

Tables

Introduction

This book is written for and about managers. It examines the phenomenon of managerial obsolescence in the context of managers themselves, their jobs and their organisations.

The book is based on a comprehensive in-depth study of managers carried out between 1977—79 and draws extensively from related work through the use of a detailed literature review.

A total of 325 managers from 138 companies were involved in the study. Eighty per cent of these were at senior or board level in their organisations and represented four functional areas: Finance, Personnel, Production and R & D. The companies included in the study had a minimum of 100 employees and represented the following sectors of industry: Engineering, Food, Drink, Tobacco, Printing and Paper. Many of the companies were multinationals, while others were native-owned.

Chapter 1 introduces the reader to the phenomenon of managerial obsolescence by examining the concept of change as it affects managers today. Reference is also made to the knowledge or information 'explosion' and finally a definition of managerial obsolescence is given.

Chapter 2 examines a variety of demographic and personal characteristics as they relate to managerial obsolescence. This and the following five chapters draw heavily from the Jones (1979) study, in the context of related research throughout the world.

Chapter 3 deals with a number of personality factors (16PF) and achievement motivation as they relate to managerial obsolescence. The importance of a positive self-concept is also examined.

Chapter 4 examines a range of job characteristics as they relate to managerial obsolescence. These include management function, level, decision-making responsibilities and job challenge.

Chapter 5 is concerned with the influences of supervisors on their subordinates' updatedness.

Chapter 6 deals with a wide range of organisational variables as they relate to managerial obsolescence. These include industrial sector, company size, company policy and organisational response to change.

Chapter 7 presents a variety of suggestions on how best to cope with or combat managerial obsolescence. It does this under three headings: the individual manager, the organisation and management development.

Chapter 8 deals with managerial obsolescence and its implications for the future. It also examines the growing practice of professional bodies who insist that their members engage in continuous updating in order to maintain accreditation.

Chapter 9 presents a summary and conclusions arising from the earlier chapters.

The book is oriented towards the practising manager in that it not only examines the factors associated with managerial obsolescence, but also presents a variety of suggestions on how to cope with or combat obsolescence.

CHAPTER 1

Defining the Problem and Nature of Obsolescence

Many terms have been used to describe the age in which we live. Some call it the 'space age', others, the 'atomic age' or the 'computer age'. Whichever title is most appropriate is uncertain, but one fact is clear — this is an age of *development and change*. It is a period in history when change seems to have speeded up, and continues to do so at an ever-increasing rate. Consequent on this is the need to keep up-to-date if one is to survive. How this is done is very much influenced by our technology, which appears, as it were, 'to feed on itself', getting larger and more complex each day, somewhat like a large tree spreading its branches and roots in all directions as it reaches up out of the earth. The difference between technology and the tree, however, is that each successive change in technology seems to render some previous change obsolete. This is evidenced by the change in the machines used each day; the electric tooth-brush at home, the cars on the road, the typewriters in the office, and the machines in the factories. When this equipment becomes obsolete it may be replaced with a more up-to-date model and so the cycle goes on. But if the

1

machine is very expensive there are a number of choices available:

1. It may be kept and its performance tolerated because it is too expensive to replace and does not justify the cost . . . yet;

2. It may be assigned to a lesser function where its limitations will not be as restrictive;

3. It may be redesigned or modified, if it is technically and economically practical;

4. It may be scrapped and replaced.

Whatever the decision, it will be influenced by a number of considerations, many of which relate to economic feasibility.

In a similar fashion, men can become obsolete. This has become evident in many spheres of life as witnessed by the mechanical digger on a construction site, operated by one man while doing the work of 50; or the process operative who controls machinery and equipment which can produce as much output in one hour as perhaps twenty manual workers could in a whole week. A further aspect of this human obsolescence is that associated with knowledge and skills. This is often a more subtle form of obsolescence, less easily identified perhaps, but no less important. The accelerative thrust of technological change has brought with it a growing need to keep abreast of the changes occurring in all branches of knowledge. The doctor, lawyer, manager, scientist or engineer, can no longer graduate from university and hope to perform his job effectively for the rest of his life without any further training or learning, as perhaps his forebears could in the past. Nowadays, continuous learning is necessary if he is to keep abreast of developments taking place in his own discipline.

Who is responsible for obsolescence? Is it the individual,

his superior, his employing organisation or his professional association? Ultimately, it is the individual himself who has to take the necessary steps to keep himself up-to-date. His superiors, employers, or professional association may play a role in this, but without individual effort it is unlikely others can help.

What of its causes? What are the factors that seem to contribute to an individual's obsolescence? Is it something about himself? The job he takes? The kind of organisation he works for? Or, is it a combination of such factors? These are some of the questions that this book seeks to answer.

This work is about the obsolescence of managers employed in industry. The focus is the obsolescence of their knowledge and skills. It is directed at managers, for they are the ones who control the making and maintenance of the machines, and goods that are used each day. They occupy key positions in organisations, and how effectively they perform their tasks will largely determine the success or otherwise of their companies. They are the ones who come face-to-face each day with changes in technology, new machinery, new processes and new products, and yet, all the time are influenced by the whims and exigencies of the market place.

CHANGES AFFECTING MANAGEMENT

There are four main types of change which make demands on managers' knowledge and skills (see Figure 1.1). The first of these is *technological change*. This is highly visible in the form of new products being created by new methods of production. Automation alone has revolutionised organisational processes, ranging from purchasing to production scheduling and control. One indication of this is the staggering increase in the use of computers. The number of computers grew from approximately 15 in the early fifties to 6,500 by 1960, passed 100,000 in 1970, and exceeds 250,000 today (Kaufman 1974). The sheer survival of many organisations is dependent on how well they respond to change, and the

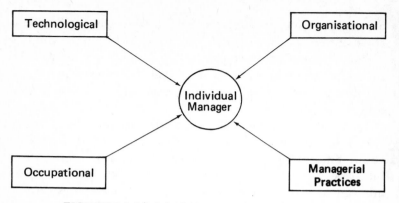

FIGURE 1.1 *Model of Changes Affecting Managers*

efforts they expend in developing innovations. Take, for instance, the introduction of plastics in the fifties. Originally plastics were seen as a poor quality substitute for wood, metal or other products, but now they have supplanted wood and metal in addition to many other substances such as glass, pottery, leather and paper in a wide variety of uses, from car bodies to packaging material.

The second major change is *occupational change.* This is clearly evidenced by the fact that workers in white-collar occupations with higher skill requirements now outnumber those in blue-collar jobs, many of which have been eliminated as a result of increased automation, mechanisation and productivity. An example of this is the increase in administrative and service sector employees, with a decline in the numbers employed in manufacturing and production. There has been a dramatic increase in the number of managerial, professional and technical personnel, which, for instance, in 1950 occupied one-tenth of the labour force in the United States, while today they represent over 25% of the working population. Under the impact of technological change, new jobs are being created while others are being changed or eliminated. An example of this is the creation of many new jobs associated with computers, from those that service them to those that operate them, plus many ancillary

4

functions such as key punch operators, programmers and data processing personnel. On the other hand, jobs such as builders and factory workers have been changed, while others are being eliminated.

Organisational change is the third major form of change which affects ever-increasing numbers of companies each year. These occur through mergers, acquisitions, development of new products, expansion of markets, especially those overseas, and the introduction of computers. Major structural changes can also be brought about by external forces such as political alliances, for example, the European Economic Community (EEC), the oil crisis of 1973 and the introduction of the European Monetary System (EMS). Planned organisational change ranging from the introduction of new management systems, various forms of organisational development programmes and the creation of new functions such as export marketing, training or R & D all play a role in most modern organisations today.

Finally, there are *changes in managerial practices*. These are reflected in the widespread use of operations research and systems analysis techniques, which emphasise quantitative and computer methodology to facilitate and improve management information, decision-making and forecasting. Management techniques also increasingly utilise behavioural science findings to improve motivation and productivity, as well as provide a more comfortable working environment for all.

The effects of these changes on the practising manager are enormous. For, besides having to cope with 'knowledge changes' in his own discipline, he must also cope with these others if he hopes to maintain his effectiveness. 'Knowledge changes' alone render particular education/training programmes of little value after a short time unless the individual continues to study and acquire new learning. The concept of *half-life*, as used in nuclear physics, has been applied to explain the rate at which a professional's knowledge goes out-of-date. When used in this context, it is a measure of the length of time after formal education/training when a professional's knowledge is only half as relevant compared to the total knowledge in his field. In some disciplines this is considered to be as low as five years (e.g. some branches of engineering), while for others it is as high as 10—12 years (e.g. psychology). Because of this, it is imperative for managers to engage in some form of continuing education/ training in order to retain the currency of knowledge and skills to meet the changing demands of their jobs. The growth in knowledge or the *knowledge revolution* has been attributed to the allocation of resources to research and development, and educational activities, which together provide the basis for the production and distribution of new knowledge, somewhat like the concept already alluded to, 'technology feeding on itself'. For instance, in the United States, funds for both R & D and education have increased at an exponential rate over the past two centuries. Machlup (1962) and Drucker (1969) both use the term *knowledge economy* to describe the phenomenon arising from the growth of the 'knowledge industries', which deal with the production and distribution of ideas and information rather than goods and services. The rapid increase in the number of knowledge workers has resulted in a staggering growth in the production and distribution of new information, sometimes referred to as the 'information explosion' (Bennet and Weiher 1972). The number of scientific journals alone has doubled every 15 years since they began 300 years ago. New books and new editions published in the United States in business, science and technology increased by 36.2% between 1950 and 1960, but by 140.3% between 1960 and 1970 (*Statistical Abstracts of the United States* 1970). To keep abreast of this newly published information, it has been estimated that 20% of a professional's working time should be devoted to reading (George and Dubin 1972). The implications of this are clear, for few professionals can afford to do this, and so the consequences are that ever-increasing numbers are becoming obsolete. The resultant effect of this

6

obsolescence for managers is a decline in performance standards, affecting industry at a time when greater demands are being made on these same industries to develop and expand. How then can industry hope to survive? What can it do to help its managers keep up-to-date? What can they do to rid themselves of structures or work practices that lead to obsolescence? Before these can be successively tackled it is first necessary to identify some of the factors that appear, as it were, to encourage or facilitate the onset of obsolescence. This book attempts to do this by examining a broad range of career, organisational and personal factors, in order to isolate those that contribute to managerial obsolescence. It is felt that by increasing our understanding of obsolescence, its causes, and antecedent effects, it will be more easily tackled in the future. It is the objective of this book to deveop this understanding of obsolescence, while at the same time providing a number of guidelines for managers and their organisations to combat and cope with its consequences.

As discussed in the Introduction, this book will be based on a large-scale study carried out by the authors on several hundred middle and senior managers in a variety of industries, and from among a number of different functions. Our intention is to weave the results of our study into existing work in the field, while at the same time providing as much data as possible to deal with the growing problem of managerial obsolescence.

DEFINITION OF OBSOLESCENCE

A problem faced by all researchers and writers in this area is that of definitions, many of which are to be found in the literature which focus on different factors underlying obsolescence. Burack and Pati (1970b), Mahler (1965), Horgan and Floyd (1971) and Shumaker (1963) have all defined obsolescence in terms of a reduction in skills or performance over time. Burack and Pati (1970b) found that managers or professionals experience obsolescence where their knowledge or skills were not adequate to meet job demands. Mahler (1975) described obsolescence as the failure of a manager to do his job with the same competence as once expected. He identified numerous categories of obsolescence, the most important of which were ability and attitude. Horgan and Floyd (1971) use two terms to describe obsolescence — *professional obsolescence* 'refers to those whose technical know-how does not include the farthest reaches of knowledge and technique which exist within their discipline', and *job obsolescence* which refers to 'a situation in which the individual's knowledge is insufficient when compared to the body of knowledge that is pertinent to the specific technical tasks that he is required to perform in his current job'. Shumaker (1963) defines obsolescence as a reduction in technical skills resulting from a manager's inability or unwillingness to keep up-to-date with new technological and other developments since leaving formal education.

Ferdinand (1966) and Norgren (1965) found several types of obsolescence when relating it to engineers and scientists. According to Ferdinand (1966):

> Obsolescence exists when an individual uses viewpoints, theories, concepts, or techniques that are less effective in solving problems than others currently available in his field of specialisation. Because he is not familiar with the best technical way of performing his assignments, the obsolete engineer or scientist takes longer in solving technical problems, and the solutions he proposes are less effective than those of his more up-to-date colleagues. Thus, he is aware of at least some of the information and techniques that are relevant to his area of responsibility, and as a result of his ignorance his work is not as useful or productive as that of others who are less obsolete.

He identifies three distinct forms of obsolescence which could affect a scientist or engineer. The first of these is termed *professional obsolescence* which refers to 'those whose technical competence does not embrace the farthest reaches of knowledge and technique comprising their discipline'. This is similar to the definition of professional obsolescence as described by Horgan and Floyd (1971). The second is termed *area obsolescence* which is 'based upon the individual's lack of knowledge of his own technical speciality'. The third type of obsolescence is called *ex officio obsolescence* and is 'that in which the individual's knowledge is compared with the body of knowledge that is relevant to the specific technical tasks he is required to perform in his current position'. Although Ferdinand (1966) distinguishes between these three forms of obsolescence, he does not state that they can and probably do converge in different individuals in a multitude of ways. His essential purpose in making these distinctions was based on his belief that remedial programmes could be most effectively implemented once the type of obsolescence was determined. Norgren (1965) on the other hand classified the major types of skill obsolescence as technology-based and product-based.

In the field of engineering, Zelikoff (1969), Mali (1970) and Siefert (1964) use the word obsolescence to refer to the erosion of the applicability of knowledge. Zelikoff (1969) analysed catalogue course offerings in five major engineering colleges in the US from 1935 to 1965 at five year intervals. By identifying courses that were added, he developed engineering erosion curves for five areas of engineering. For instance, in the case of electrical engineers in 1965, the percentage of applicable knowledge was about 5% for the class of 1935 compared to about 55% for the class of 1960. Mali (1970) developed what he called the obsolescence index (OI) in order to define the concept of obsolescence:

$$OI = \frac{\text{Current knowledge understood by the individual}}{\text{Current knowledge in the field}}$$

For OI to remain constant with time, the denominator and numerator must change at the same fractional rate, but in reality the denominator grows exponentially in time. As the equation is based on the rate of change versus time, high

9

rates of technical obsolescence are related to high rates of growth.

According to Siefert (1964), 'obsolescence is the measurement at some point in time of the difference between the knowledge and skills possessed by the practising professional who may have completed his formal education a number of years previously, and those possessed by a recent graduate of a modern curriculum'. Other writers have also contributed to the discussion such as Haas (1968), Kaufman (1974) and Dubin (1972).

Some of these definitions refer to knowledge only (Mali 1970) or skill (Shumaker 1963 and Norgren 1965), while others combine knowledge and skill (Burack and Pati 1970b and Siefert 1964). Since skill refers to the application of knowledge which seems to be implied by these writers, then it is important for managers to have both relevant and adequate knowledge and skills if they are to work effectively. A lack of either will lead to obsolescence in terms of the job managers have to perform. It is not essential for a manager to have all the technical know-how relevant to his discipline in order to perform a particular job well, for no single job requires this breadth of knowledge and skills. Hence, Horgan and Floyd's (1971) definition of 'Professional Obsolescence' appears unrealistic in terms of a professional's work; Ferdinand's (1966) definition refers to out-of-date viewpoints, theories, concepts and techniques, but how he defines out-of-dateness is not clear. If one examines any industry or job it is almost certain one will find a variety of theories, concepts, and techniques in practice, some more modern than others, yet, not necessarily more effective. Is the use of wheels, gears, steam, electricity etc. out-of-date? True, they are not modern, but yet we depend on them greatly for modern technology. The definition of Burack and Pati (1970b) is considered to be the most relevant to this book which is concerned with managers and their jobs within an industrial context.

Most of the definitions outlined above were mainly

referring to engineers and scientists but since this book is
about managers, which of course may include engineers and
scientists but not exclusively so, it was necessary to develop
a definition which would have more general application.
The following is this definition as used for the purposes of
this research study and book.

> *Managerial obsolescence* is defined, for the purpose of this study,
> as the extent to which a manager's knowledge and skills have failed
> to keep pace with the current and likely future requirements of
> his job.

This definition then, includes that of Burack and Pati
(1970b) while extending that of Mahler (1965) and en-
compassing Horgan and Floyd's (1971) definition of 'job
obsolescence'.

CHAPTER 2

Personal Characteristics which Affect Managerial Obsolescence

There are many personal characteristics which are likely to influence or affect a manager's updatedness. This chapter will deal with the following characteristics for they are felt to be the most important: Age, Educational Qualifications, Work Experience and Mobility, Perception of Learning Ability, Learning Ability and Age, Attitude to the Importance of Updating, Type of Updating Activity Engaged In and Membership of Professional Associations. (See Figure 2.1.)

For detailed statistical information on the relationship between these variables and different aspects of obsolescence e.g. relevance and adequacy of managers' knowledge and skills and transferability of skills, see Appendix 2.

MANAGER'S AGE

Research on obsolescence, performance ratings and learning ability in relation to age has yielded much contradictory evidence. Some researchers maintain that age is an important determinant of performance and learning ability, and hence a factor in obsolescence, while others maintain the opposite.

Significant	Not Significant
Age	Educational & professional/ technical qualifications
Work experience	
Mobility	Type of updating activities engaged in
Perception of their learning ability	
Attitude to importance of updating	
Membership of professional associations	

FIGURE 2.1 *Personal Characteristics Related to Managerial Obsolescence*

Lehman (1963) established that men in certain kinds of intellectual careers, particularly in the sciences, had their most productive years in the early part of their careers. Pelz and Andrews (1966) also reported this to be the case for engineers.

Dalton and Thompson (1971) found a negative correlation between age and performance ranking after age 35. They report that there was a significant relationship between age and performance, where average rankings were higher for each age group until the early 30's and then successively lower for each group until retirement. In later research, they report that seniority in itself did not automatically indicate fading capability. Veteran engineers who were rated highly by their superiors held their own against younger competitors (Thompson *et al.* 1974). Rankings of engineers' or managers' performance are important because they are often used as the basis for determining promotions, salary increases, job assignments and so forth. In their examination of salaries, Dalton and Thompson (1971) found that while performance rankings begin to fall after the mid-thirties, salaries continue to climb until the early forties before levelling off. This has serious implications for mobility within an organisation, for the older manager who feels that he is not highly valued will tend to cling to his high-salaried job instead of seeking another one where his talents may be better appreciated. When examining how managers and engineers looked at performance and age, they found that for engineers who stayed in technical jobs their most sophisticated work was done at age 37, while for those who moved into management it was at age 47. The greatest effort on the part of the engineer was at 35, while for managers it was in their early 40's. Their major concern, resulting from research carried out over an extended period, is that the years of high performance (at least of *recognised* high performance) seem to be starting and ending sooner than they were even a few years ago, and that this shift is occurring when large numbers of technical personnel are entering their 40's and 50's.

A different perspective was presented in the conclusion to a study of 'performance as a function of age', where A.J. Bernstein (Manager of Professional Personnel at the General Electric Research Centre) found that there is no significant relationship between age and value to the company. This is because although there is a slight falling-off of productivity, as measured by patents and publications, it is counterbalanced by other factors such as judgement, contracts in the company and influence on other employees, which also benefit the company. He also firmly believes from his investigation that an 'ageing poor performer' has, in almost all cases, been a poor performer from early in his career and should have been redirected or terminated earlier. Van Atta *et al.* (1970) report that there is considerable evidence in support of the belief that, given a stimulating environment conducive to productive effort, including opportunities for educational renewal and a diversity of work experience, well-motivated scientists and engineers will maintain productivity up to the normal retirement age of 65 years, unless failing health becomes an obstacle. A review of literature on ageing carried out by Van Atta *et al.* (1970) concludes that:

14

1. In scientific research activities, creative contributions of major significance most generally occur before the age of 40. In developmental scientific activities, the majority of more significant contributions occur before the age of 50;

2. During mid-career, between the 40's and early 50's, there may be a tendency to 'coast';

3. After age 50, productivity tends to climb because they are generally secure in their positions, have fewer family pressures and are willing to take risks;

4. Engineers tend to improve with age if the work depends on the breadth and depth of the technical experience and not so much on creativeness. However, in a field in which there are rapid changes, improvement may depend more upon learning new technologies than upon on-the-job experience;

5. Studies reveal that intellectual capability declines little with age;

6. The most crucial determinants of productivity and creativity are motivation and opportunity;

7. Outstanding performers are those who are highly motivated and evidence a large measure of self-confidence in their work;

8. There is strong evidence that superiors should stress continuing education, assignment rotation and the like, for their subordinates;

9. Since there is often a decline in performance after age 40, it would seem appropriate to consider setting up mid-career reviews for professionals.

Burack and Pati (1970a, b) identified a number of factors conducive to managerial obsolescence: lack of awareness of change, aptitude to learn, outdated education, lack of motivation for self-education because of age and low level of aspiration. Miller (1974) and Farris (1973) also comment on age as a factor influencing managers' willingness to participate in career development programmes. However, not much has been documented on this topic in relation to management.

In terms of obsolescence ratings in our study, we found that older managers rated themselves the least obsolete, while younger ones rated themselves the most obsolete. This trend was maintained between the age groups, but it was not possible to check whether it held true within each age group. The importance of this finding is that it both refutes the hypothesis that younger managers would be less likely to experience high levels of obsolescence, and also contradicts the findings of Dalton and Thompson (1971), Vollmer and McAuliff (1968) and others. Age in itself appears to be a significant factor in relation to obsolescence. It may also be important in association with other factors such as learning ability, attitude to updating and participation in updating activities. Perhaps the reason why age is so significant is because of the belief that, given a stimulating environment with plenty of job challenge and an opportunity to engage in updating activities, well-motivated managers will continue to remain productive up to retirement age.

A further point is that older managers have developed a variety of strategies to cope with change and new developments, and have the experience necessary to gain from the up-to-date knowledge and skills of younger staff. Perhaps, also, because they are generally at more senior levels, they do not require the same level of technical expertise as more junior managers do, in that their jobs tend to be orientated more towards policy-making, administration and co-ordination of staff, rather than the application of direct technical knowledge. This is more often left to middle- and first-line management staff.

MANAGER'S EDUCATIONAL & PROFESSIONAL/ TECHNICAL QUALIFICATIONS

A problem faced by all managers is that related to the currency of their educational and professional/technical knowledge. Once managers leave formal education/training, they must then rely on their own self-education strategies

16

for updating. The trouble with these is that they are unlikely to be either as systematic or comprehensive as those they have left. This results in managers becoming increasingly out-of-date, for knowledge continues to grow at an ever-expanding rate, while their learning will tend to decrease with time. Raudsepp (1964b) explains this using the term *felt obsolescence* and indicates that although managers' knowledge and skills might be going out-of-date, they will be influenced by the type of jobs they have. If they have a challenging job requiring the use of existing knowledge and skills, together with the development of new knowledge and skills, they will remain up-to-date longer than those who work in more routine jobs or those who move into administration.

Perrucci and Rothman (1969) reported that education and experience influence vulnerability to obsolescence. They found in the case of engineers, that those with advanced degrees exhibited significantly less obsolescence than those with only a bachelors degree. They also found that the highest levels of obsolescence were experienced by those in administrative positions, while the lowest were experienced by those in research and development positions. They also reported that limited technical responsibility increased vulnerability to obsolescence, by allowing the degeneration of existing knowledge through disuse, and failing to stimulate self-education because it was not necessary.

The managers in our study were generally highly qualified in that two-thirds of them had some form of third level qualification, the most common of which was some kind of certificate or diploma. 44% of those with third level qualifications had degrees, the most common of which were BA and BComm.; whereas 10% had post-graduate degrees, mainly at the masters level. Managers in the larger companies were more likely to have a degree than those in the smaller companies. The highest proportion of degree holders were in the Food, Drink and Tobacco companies, while the lowest were in Engineering companies. R & D managers were the best qualified academically, followed by Production, Personnel and Finance. Junior and senior managers were the most highly qualified but the further up the hierarchical ladder, the lower the proportion of post-graduate degrees possessed by managers.

The reason why Food, Drink and Tobacco companies had the highest proportion of degrees is because many managers in these industries require a high technical background in terms of chemistry, biochemistry and various branches of biology. In the case of Engineering and Printing and Paper companies, many managers had come up through the ranks having completed some form of craft apprenticeship rather than a university course.

R & D followed by Production managers were the most highly qualified because these were the ones who required a high level of technical expertise in order to do their job well. Personnel and Financial managers, on the other hand, tended to acquire professional qualifications such as IPM, ACCA, ACMA or ACA rather than take some university course. They did, however, tend to continue studying further into their careers than R & D or Production managers, for their qualifications were often more dependent on job experience. Many of the managers in Personnel and Finance in our study had continued taking courses into their 30's in order to gain a professional qualification. They indicated that this was necessary if their qualifications were to be of any value to their work. Managers in R & D and Production were generally ones who went through university and got their degrees before starting out in their careers, or else did an apprenticeship in the early part of their job and progressed from there. This difference in preparation for careers between the functions has important implications in terms of obsolescence. For, the longer people study, the longer they delay obsolescence and so keep up-to-date, whereas if they complete their studies before taking up a job, then they will become vulnerable to obsolescence early in their careers. This is also shown by the fact that there was no consistency between level of qualification and degree of obsolescence in our study. This was demonstrated by the fact that those with third level certificates/diplomas rated themselves more up-to-date than those with masters degrees or BE/BSc degrees.

The fact that the junior and senior managers were the most highly qualified, possibly reflects the fact that, in the case of junior managers, they were younger and hence had greater educational opportunities than older managers; whereas senior managers who did get to the top were perhaps those who were well qualified to start with. This finding corroborates that of Kaufman (1974), who found that highly qualified managers (engineers) tend to stay abreast of their disciplines better than less qualified ones and also progress further.

It was not surprising to find that managers in Finance and Personnel were mainly qualified in these respective disciplines, while those in Production and R & D were mainly qualified in engineering and science. Board level and senior managers were qualified mainly in Finance, while for middle managers it was Engineering, followed by Personnel. These results suggest that Finance is an important qualification in terms of promotion, but may it also say something more than this? Perhaps it is true that since Finance is a subject studied by managers long into their careers, they are better able to keep up-to-date than managers in other disciplines, and hence get to the top faster. In fact, our results indicate that those qualified in Finance, Science and Technology rated themselves lower on obsolescence than any of the others.

MANAGER'S WORK EXPERIENCE AND MOBILITY

There are many assumptions made by managers who feel that the longer the work experience or the more mobility a manager has had, the more up-to-date he must be. These are not always true, for many managers with many years experience may have had these in a very limited job or company. Hence, they may be expert as far as their particular job is concerned, and even this is not always true, but they may be hopelessly out-of-date relative to colleagues in other disciplines or companies.

What motivates a manager to become mobile? Many reasons are given in the literature. Roche (1975) claims they are seeking 'self-actualisation' rather than money. Immundo (1974) indicates that it is more to do with the high task and achievement orientation of managers for whom movement becomes an end in itself. Others say that 'travel is the hall-mark of success' (Seidenberg 1973) or as Jennings (1967) puts it in relation to top American executives, 'the manager who centres his life-style upon mobility is the conformist' and advocates that both he and his family learn to like this state of affairs. Further substantiating evidence comes from the complementary claim by Morris (1956) that research has shown 'more psychosomatic illness from being passed over' than from achieving high management positions.

Of course many managers have no choice in the matter as evidenced in House's (1969) study, where 25% of moves were compulsory within company relocations. A further complication is that workers' motivations may well change with situations and over time. Daniel (1972), for example, reviews several research studies carried out on production workers' motivations during collective bargaining. These suggest that whilst earnings and workload were the main preoccupations during negotiations, job enrichment and security became dominant elements in the later assessment of the value of the agreement.

Literature such as the BIM report *The Management Threshold* and *Men in Mid-Career* (Sofer 1970) suggest that managers' work motivations develop with their careers. In the early career-formation stage it appears that employees devote more time and energy to their jobs (sometimes at the expense of their home life) and it is likely that they will be more willing to move to better their prospects. As managers move into mid-career, monetary rewards become less important as mastery of the job becomes their prime focus. Coming up to retirement there is a further change in emphasis as managers invest more of their time and energy in out-of-work activities. This may be to compensate for having reached their 'career ceiling' and tends to make them less willing to move away.

According to Sleeper (1975) who used unpublished British statistics for the period 1960—66, younger workers are highly mobile as they search for training, career prospects and (when married) higher incomes. However, mobility drops off as the worker stands to gain from the seniority system in his company and as the skills he has developed are less transferable to new employers. A rise in mobility for those nearing retirement, he suggests, is a search for higher jobs and more flexible hours.

Mobility may be an effective way of keeping a manager up-to-date, but this is only when the various career changes are well planned and executed. A manager who readily changes jobs every couple of years may be only avoiding rough situations. 'When the going gets tough move on', is not a very effective way of keeping abreast of new developments in one's field. Likewise, many managers may be forced to move about through what Daniel (1970) calls 'galloping redundancy'. This arises when a manager, after experiencing his first job loss, often experiences many more, for he falls foul of the often used strategy of 'last in, first out' approach of companies instituting redundancies.

Mant (1969) suggests that mobility among managers is a response to lack of job challenge or frustration in their careers. Furthermore, Hanson (1977) indicates that this leads to a demand for more effective career development and career planning. Wool (1973) and Blood and Hulin (1967) found that when managers had low morale and were frustrated in their careers, they were forced to do something to restimulate themselves, this often leading to career changes as a way of coping with the problem. However, it does not appear to be an effective way of coping with managerial

21

obsolescence. Perhaps this is because obsolescence is a more deep-rooted problem, which requires ongoing development, rather than a sudden job change which may not necessarily help the individual at all in terms of his/her professional growth.

In terms of our particular study, managers' work experience and mobility were found to be significantly related to some aspects of obsolescence, namely relevance and adequacy of knowledge, but were not significantly related to managers' skills. These results indicate that work experience and mobility are not so important in relation to managerial obsolescence.

MANAGER'S PERCEPTION OF HIS LEARNING ABILITY

The results of our study show that 'up-to-date managers' had a positive perception of their learning ability, enjoyed new learning experiences and felt that their learning ability had improved in recent years. In fact, this hypothesis is the only one which was fully upheld by our study (which indicates its importance). Perhaps this is because managers who feel that they are learners, or capable of learning, are more willing to engage in new learning experiences, either in a formal (course) or informal (on-the-job) setting. They will take on the challenge of new work demands. Perrucci and Rothman (1969) conclude, that 'those managers who engaged in learning experiences long into their careers were the least likely to become obsolete'. This, of course, is moving into the realm of continuous or lifelong education which Ansoff (1973) suggests is an integral part of future management education. Managers will no longer rely solely on episodic or passive learning, but will move to 'career long' and active/participative learning. This in turn will create new demands on management educators and trainers who in turn will be encouraged to develop new strategies or

22

methods of facilitating learning, such as suggested by Burgoyne and Stuart (1978).

Some recent developments in this area have been made by Morris (1975a, b), Revans (1971) and Boxer (1975). Managers themselves also need to develop their own learning approaches, for as Mant (1969) indicates, they must ultimately take responsibility for their own learning. They must learn to cope with change (Toffler 1970) and learn to benefit from their experience in a self-directed way in line with the philosophy of Rogers (1969).

LEARNING ABILITY AND AGE

Until recently it was thought that learning ability and performance declined with age. This was often attributed either to changes in the sense organs, muscles and joints or to changes of interest, so that older people were less able at activities such as mental arithmetic or languages or indeed learning generally, because it was so long since they had been required to perform these tasks at school (Welford 1976). One of the central factors influencing changes with age can be attributed to a lowering of signal to noise ratio in the brain. This was found to be due both to a loss of sensitivity of sense organs and to losses of active brain cells so that signal strengths are reduced. It is also partly due to increased random activity within the brain, so called 'neural noise' (Crossman and Szafran 1956, Gregory 1974, Welford 1962 and 1965). This fall in signal to noise ratio leads to slower performance and increased tendency to error. Older people have, however, been found to compensate by accumulating data over a longer period of time and thus strengthening the signal and reducing or neutralising some of the noise before making a decision (e.g. Botwinick, Brinley and Robbin 1958, Vickers, Nettleback and Wilson 1972).

The result of this is slower performance but less error. Older people are also known to take more care over their

23

work than younger ones and strive for greater accuracy (Welford 1958 and 1976, Botwinick 1966, Craik 1969). Their learning is marked by features of continuous searching, exploration and integration (Belbin 1969).

Memory is another factor which appears to be influenced by age. It appears that immediate memory involves the co-operation of a short-term and a long-term store (Waugh and Norman 1965, Welford 1968) and that older people have difficulty registering material rapidly in the longer-term store. Rehearsal is one way of counteracting learning difficulties among older people (Speakman, *see* Welford 1958). Another problem with memory is the difficulty in recovering material from long-term store. In response to this problem, older people tend to adopt one of two strategies: either they make 'no recall' rather than hazard a guess, or alternatively they attempt to respond and risk errors; both of these strategies have been found (Korchin and Basowitz 1957, Brunning, Holzbauer and Kimberlin 1975). These two trends appear to account for much of the difficulty shown by older people in learning. This is because the essential problem of learning for older people lies in the acquisition and recovery of material rather than in its retention, but some of these problems can be overcome with suitable methods of training (Belbin 1964, Belbin 1965, Belbin and Downs 1966, Chown, Belbin and Downs 1967).

Rogers (1970) points out that contrary to popular belief, memory in general does not grow appreciably worse as people get older, but an important change does take place which affects ability to learn. Short-term memory capacity begins to decline so that information received is often confused and forgotten if new information comes flooding in soon afterwards. This has implications for teaching methods such as lectures and demonstrations. The older people grow, the less they are able to learn by being told things, and it looks as though many of the traditional failures of adult learners are due to a 'short-circuiting' in the brain which cannot sort out verbal information quickly enough. Research has shown that when adults do not have to rely on spoken words or demonstrations and are allowed to learn through their own activity, the improvement in performance can be startling (Rogers 1970).

In reference to training objectives it is not unusual to find that they are expressed in terms of what instructors or course designers want, rather than in terms of what the trainees require. As a result, trainees are often not sure what is expected of them and even when told by instructors, some doubts and ambiguities remain. If the training material is not relevant to trainees' needs it may become superfluous. Rogers (1971) states that adults like to feel that what they are learning is going to be useful and relevant in their daily lives and they also learn more rapidly the closer the resemblance between the learning task and the skill they finally hope to attain.

Knowledge of results is also an important feature in adult learning. The adult needs to know how he has performed soon after completing a task. Since, as Powell (1969) puts it, 'for success in practice the learner must want to succeed, he must succeed and he must know that he has succeeded'. Belbin and Belbin (1972) point out that the performance skills required in *training* differ somewhat from those required in *production*. They state that:

> performance in training often demands a high verbal comprehension, a retentive and flexible mind and a capacity for sustained concentration. Performance in production, on the other hand, commonly calls for applied effort, reliability and conscientiousness in ensuring quality of work, ingenuity in coping with difficulties, and such social assets as a capacity for team work.

The following findings, reported by Belbin (1969), summarise the results of four studies on adult learning:

1. In a comparison of teaching methods with age, it was found that under 30's did better on programmed instruction while over 30's did better on the traditional methods.

25

2. Older trainees did better when allowed to 'discover' rather than being 'explained and demonstrated to' by a skilled and experienced instructor. The discovery method improves the learning achievement of adults and the relative gain is usually greater for the older adult.

3. Mature adults do not react very favourably towards imitative types of learning, such as the learning of language fluency.

The conclusion drawn from these findings is that in planning training programmes for older adults it is useful to distinguish between forms of learning to decide which are being developed, and to determine whether the methods used are appropriate to the aims and to the propensities of the learners.

Recent work by Piotr Anokbin of Moscow University (see Buzan 1977) suggests that the creative potential in everyone is virtually limitless. Further work by Rosenzweiz found that the brain was more 'plastic' than had been previously envisioned, and that this plasticity remained throughout a lifetime. These results contradicted the previous assumptions that as the brain got older it automatically deteriorated. According to Buzan, the implications of this research for commerce and industry are clear:

> that our practice of slotting people into specific jobs, and of assuming they must be retired at an early age, is probably counter-productive. Rather, we should be considering massive retraining programmes and a more sensible use of these people who have been trained and have a major degree of experience and skill.

Hence, although older adults may have less energy and sometimes suffer from physical handicaps such as reduced use of their senses, they do make up for much of these in their increased ability to concentrate, and patience in

26

learning new work patterns. As a result they are often as capable and, indeed, sometimes more capable of benefiting from training than younger workers.

ATTITUDE TO THE IMPORTANCE OF UPDATING

The importance of updating and *motivation* to keep abreast of developments in his/her field are two complex factors of a manager's life. Many managers do not realise the need to keep up-to-date because of the job they hold. If they are in an administrative function, they may not need to worry as much about technological change as if they were in a technical job. The need to keep in touch with new management practices and procedures does not always influence managers, for many continue to carry out their duties as 'tradition dictates' or as they are instructed, and as long as their companies continue to make profits they see little need for change. The difficulty with this is that out-of-date routines are often adhered to long after their usefulness has become undermined. For example, we found a number of cases of financial managers who were still using cumbersome and archaic book-keeping procedures which require a great deal of manpower, when they could have streamlined their operation by introducing modern computer-based accountancy procedures. Similar out-of-date procedures are often maintained within the production function, when they could be improved by using, for instance, production scheduling and control.

The results of our study showed that *up-to-date managers* indicated that it was important to keep abreast of new developments in their particular field of interest, both to maintain effectiveness in their present jobs and also to help in the development of their careers. Without actively engaging in updating activities they felt that they would not be able to cope effectively with changes in their jobs and would be unlikely to progress their careers very far.

TYPE OF UPDATING ACTIVITY ENGAGED IN

Managers in our study were provided with a list of updating activities that they might engage in and were asked to score those that they had participated in and how effective they felt them to be. (See Figure 2.2.)

The results indicated that participation in any of the updating activities was not significantly related to any of the obsolescence variables. Perhaps the reason for this is that participation in updating activities in itself is not so important in terms of managerial obsolescence. It may be more important to have a positive disposition or orientation to updating. In other words, it may be more a question of engaging in lifelong education than in sporadic courses, seminars or workshops. A further point of note is the fact

---

In-Company Training Programmes

Job-Related External Training Programmes

Secondment to Other Organisations

Job Rotation Within Own Organisation

Educational Leave

On-the-job Problem-Solving

Attendance at Professional Society Meetings

Seminars/Conferences

Reading Work-Related Books

Reading Work-Related Journals

Educational Programmes in Own Time

FIGURE 2.2 *List of Updating Activities*

that the supplied list may not have been comprehensive enough or perhaps was based too much on formal activities such as courses, seminars and meetings.

The most commonly practised updating activities for all managers were: reading work-related books and journals, on-the-job problem-solving and attending seminars and conferences. Many writers have found that on-the-job problem-solving was the most important aid in helping managers to keep abreast of developments in their field (Margulies and Raia 1967). Kaufman (1974) emphasises the same point from his research and goes on to suggest that if a manager's job is not challenging and stimulating, then it should be redesigned and enriched.

Although many managers in our study read work-related books and journals, these were not found to be very helpful in keeping them up-to-date. This is explained by some who said that they often only skimmed through the journals. One manager put it this way, 'I get a lot of journals here and they just sit on my desk for weeks. When I get a spare minute I may glance through one or two or even take one home with me, but I rarely sit down and read them'. Another said, 'I do not get to read them at the office and I do not like taking them home as the wife does not like me reading technical journals there. She feels that should be done at the office'.

The most highly rated updating activities were educational programmes that managers followed in their own time, and on-the-job problem-solving. The least helpful were attendance at professional society meetings and reading work-related books and journals.

Younger managers were the most likely to engage in educational programmes in their own time as they saw this as an opportunity to gain qualifications in such areas as personnel and finance, or even do an MBA degree. Older managers who took education courses, usually did so in languages, especially French and German, which they saw to be important for their jobs.

Vollmer and McAuliffe (1968) report that 80% of the companies in their study indicated that they experienced increasing pressure from managers to engage in updating activities in recent years. The most common activities were: university courses (90%), internal and external seminars (85%), in-house updating courses (80%) and maintaining libraries on management subjects (75%). In an AMA (1968) study of executive obsolescence, it was reported that 50% of the companies used continuing education, executive promotions, rotation and demotion to help managers keep up-to-date.

Dalton and Thompson (1971) and Evan (1963) put forward the idea of industrial sabbaticals as a useful means for helping managers keep up-to-date. This was based on the finding that engineers who completed post-graduate degrees were less prone to obsolescence than their colleagues.

It appears that the methods used by American companies are more diverse than those used by Irish or UK companies, but perhaps this is due to the difference in culture and orientation of their respective managers.

MEMBERSHIP OF PROFESSIONAL ASSOCIATIONS

Membership of professional associations was found to be significantly related to obsolescence. Our results suggest that this is an important way of helping managers cope with or prevent the onset of obsolescence.

Two-thirds of our sample held a total of 328 memberships of professional associations (see list of Associations in Appendix 2). Some managers were members of up to four different associations. The most common were those associated with finance (43%) and personnel and training (22%). Rothman and Perrucci (1971) report that obsolescence tends to decrease as the extent of involvement in professional activities increases. Haas (1968) indicates that membership of professional associations is an important factor in helping managers to keep up-to-date. However, the results of our study indicate that attendance at professional society meetings is not found to be helpful in maintaining updatedness.

This was particularly true of non-financial associations. As one manager put it, 'those meetings are really only an excuse to get together with the boys for a good meal and a booze-up afterwards'. Many indicated that the meetings were primarily social get-togethers. They suggested that professional associations faced a dilemma in that, if they put on a good educational programme with guest speakers no one would go, while if they put on a social function then everyone went. Financial associations were felt to be much better at organising their members and providing attractive meetings with interesting topics and speakers. These were well-attended and found to be beneficial to members in terms of providing useful input on complex topics. They also provided a forum for discussion of common financial problems.

CHAPTER 3

Personality Factors and Achievement Needs in Relation to Obsolescence

PERSONALITY

There has been little research done to study the relationship between personality factors and obsolescence. Yet, Gaudet and Carli (1957) report that personality factors have been identified as the major cause of failure among managers. Two aspects of personality have been found to be important determinants of managerial obsolescence: (1) the individual's self-concept, and (2) the way in which he responds to change (Kaufman 1974). When managers learn that they can effectively master the challenges of their environment, feelings of competence, self-esteem, and confidence emerge as integral parts of their self-concepts (Hall 1971). The converse is also true in that, those who fail to master their environment experience feelings of low competence, low self-esteem and low self-confidence. An individual's self-esteem will influence both his occupational choice and his level of career success. Kaufman (1974) also indicates that it will influence his attitude and behaviour towards keeping up-to-date, which in effect influences his vulnerability to obsolescence.

Those with a high self-esteem will generally seek new ways to keep abreast of developments in their field and set goals which will demand high levels of performance. Those with low self-esteem will take the opposite route. This is often because they are more concerned with security/safety needs than they are with growth needs. Kaufman (1974) has found that professionals who begin their careers with high self-assurance are significantly more satisfied with their attainment of professional aspirations and recognition, as well as management aspirations, later on in their careers, than are those who have low self-esteem. This predisposition to career growth/success is thought to play an important role on determining whether or not professionals become obsolescent. The professional who sets out with a positive self-concept will be likely to take on new challenges, seek diversity of work, and broaden his skills early in his career. Thus, success leads to more sucess, and so he progresses up the hierarchical ladder with little difficulty. On the other hand, the professional with low self-esteem will more likely take on familiar jobs, not take risks and so not broaden his skills, thus leading to a stable, but unprogressive, career. He is likely to avoid 'updating activities' for fear of failure and hence become susceptible to obsolescence. This then leads to greater doubts about his abilities and hence a greater desire to protect his job at the expense of development — a destructive obsolescence feedback loop, a vicious unending circle.

With the growing need for change in organisations, as a result of work restructuring, new technology, new markets and products etc., it has become essential for managers to be able to cope with change if they are to remain viable and productive. A key element of an individual's ability to cope with change is his willingness to take risks (Argyris 1965). The fear of taking any risks has, in fact, been identified by managers as an important contributing cause of obsolescence.

Rogers (1962), who has studied the relationship between an individual's openness to new ideas and innovations, suggests that '. . . venturesomeness is almost an obsession with innovators. They are eager to try new ideas'. Managers who hope to succeed must keep abreast of new developments and be prepared to take risks, and not fear failure (which is an integral offshoot of risk-taking behaviour).

Some research indicates that risk-taking behaviour is influenced by age. Young managers are likely to take many risks early in their careers for they have little to lose; this is followed by a more cautious period when the manager has established himself and is unwilling to take too many chances. However, this can change towards the latter end of a manager's career when he has become well established, has reached his career-ceiling and hence does not fear the consequences of failure anymore, and so begins to take risks again.

Another important characteristic associated with obsolescence is *rigidity,* which can impair a manager's ability to cope with change (McKinnon 1962). This is often exemplified in managers who try to cope with change by ignoring it or continuing to use old, out-of-date procedures to deal with it. Some executives have identified this reluctance to change as an important factor contributing to obsolescence. The opposite of this is openness to new ideas, originality and creativity. These are associated with flexibility and ability to 'take change in one's stride'.

A further factor which has been found to influence managerial susceptibility to obsolescence is intelligence. In fact, Kaufman (1974) goes so far as to state 'inadequate cognitive ability is the most important personal characteristic that predisposes a professional to obsolescence'. His research indicates that the higher a manager's intellectual ability at the outset of his/her career, the more likely he/she is to keep up-to-date. Those with low intellectual ability tend to go into jobs which do not demand a high level of cognitive skills. This often leads to lack of use, resulting in a negative perception of their own learning ability. This, of course, tends to frighten managers from attending courses or seminars for instance, and so they rapidly go out-of-date and become obsolescent. Many have felt that intellectual ability tends to decrease with age, but this is refuted by the work of Minor (1969) and Buzan (1977), as discussed earlier.

ACHIEVEMENT MOTIVATION

Achievement motivation is a further factor which appears to influence susceptibility to managerial obsoleseence (Reeser 1977, Rothman and Perrucci 1971, Levene 1976, Dubin 1972, Hall 1971 and Kaufman 1974). According to Levene (1976) those managers with *high achievement needs* will tend to move into dynamic growth-orientated organisations and will constantly seek new challenges and goals. Those with *low achievement needs* will tend to gravitate towards more structured organisations such as government bodies or large multinational companies.

Achievement motivation, as described by Atkinson and Feather (1966), is an index of generalised motivation for achievement involving desire for success and fear of failure. Persons who are highly motivated are generally attracted to activities which require skill and excellence in performance. McClelland and Winters (1969) found that high levels of achievement motivation are associated with entrepreneurial behaviour, innovative risk-taking, and business success. Men with a high need to achieve tend to:

1. Seek and assume a high degree of personal responsibility;

2. Take moderate or calculated risks;

3. Set challenging but realistic goals for themselves;

4. Develop comprehensive plans to attain their goals;

5. Show preference for problem situations which provide concrete measurable feedback of their performance;

6. Seek out business opportunities where their desire to achieve will not be thwarted;

7. Spend time thinking about how to get things done better and take pride in accomplishment; and

8. Show more initiative and exploratory behaviour by continually researching the environment to find tasks they can solve to their satisfaction.

(McClelland and Winter 1969).

Stringer (1966), on the other hand, suggests that a person's achievement depends on both his motives and his environment. His motivation depends on:

1. the strength of the motive;

2. the person's expectation that he can satisfy the motive; and

3. the amount of satisfaction he anticipates.

Task competence is also related to motivation (Bass 1970). He describes the task-orientated person as being 'persistent, confident, objective, intelligent and single minded'. These qualities appear to be goal- and achievement-orientated, and characteristic of those who wish to remain up-to-date. Kaufman (1974) reports on a study which found that among computer, marketing and support personnel at a senior management level, a lack of motivation was the most frequently cited factor in an individual's becoming out-of-date.

Motivation in itself is a rather broad concept and can be broken down into different aspects such as interests, needs, goals, energy and initiative. Interests not only help to determine occupational choice but also influence managers' job function, level of responsibility, performance, and innovativeness (Benjamin 1967). This is exemplified by the fact that managers with a high 'interest in people' tend to go

36

into jobs with a high degree of personal contact, while those more interested in ideas or things tend to go into jobs such as quality control, costing, research and development, etc. These job differences influence the utilisation of managerial skills and abilities, and hence vulnerability to obsolescence. Interests in keeping up-to-date and engaging in updating activities have obvious implications for obsolescence.

Need changes also effect obsolescence in that managers who have a high *need to achieve* are more likely to remain up-to-date than those with the opposite. Need achievement is well documented in the work of Maslow (1943), McGregor (1960) and Hertzberg *et al.* (1959). When a manager starts out in his career he has a high need to establish himself securely, and to make a mark on the organisation. Later his needs shift to *esteem* and *achievement.* The stronger these are, the less vulnerable he is to obsolescence, because he is more dependent on his own skills, is willing to take risks, assumes greater responsibility for decision-making and seeks opportunities for growth. When these needs are satisfied, the manager may then move to satisfy higher order needs by getting involved in professional associations, local politics, community services, etc. Managers' goals also change with time during their careers. It has been found, for instance, that some managers when they embark on their careers have a desire to achieve higher academic or professional qualifications, while others' goals are to progress up the hierarchical ladder. Those who are interested in professional goals are known as 'cosmopolitans', while those interested in organisational goals are known as 'locals'. Kaufman (1974) has found that 'cosmopolitans' are generally less *obsolescence-prone* than 'locals'. This is because they seek to keep up-to-date with changes in their profession/discipline, while 'locals' are more concerned with organisational matters and hence let their professional skills get out-of-date. Goals, of course, change over time with career progress, so that there may be changes in emphasis from 'cosmopolitan' to 'local' or *vice versa*, at different stages in an individual's career. Indeed, a single individual usually has a mixture of goals to start with; it is the emphasis placed on them that tends to distinguish one manager from the other. A study by Ritzer and Trice (1969) on personnel managers found that because personnel administration, as an occupation, is part bureaucratic and part professional, they are committed both to the occupation and the organisation. In other words, personnel managers supplement their commitment to the occupation with some degree of commitment to the organisation.

A number of studies indicate that managers who have a large amount of energy available for their work, tend to use it on their careers as well as intellectual pursuits to keep up-to-date (Kaufman 1974).

Chambers (1964) suggests that personal initiative is related to energy level and so contributes to the expenditure of energy on updating activities. Initiative involves not only the beginning of actions, but also the capacity to note and discover new means of goal attainment. The manager with a high degree of initiative is able to pursue goals and take action to achieve them without resorting to stimulation or help from others.

PERSONALITY CHARACTERISTICS OF OBSOLESCENT VERSUS NON—OBSOLESCENT MANAGERS

In our study we examined the personality of both the obsolescent and non-obsolescent managers in the study. This was done to find out what, if any, relationship there was between personality and obsolescence.

We hypothesised that managers with different levels of obsolescence would have different personality profiles. The high obsolescence scoring managers were hypothesised to be reserved, less intelligent, affected by feelings, humble, sober, expedient, shy, tender-minded, suspicious, imaginative, forthright, apprehensive, conservative, group-dependent, tense, and have an undisciplined self-concept and a low level of achievement. The low obsolescence scoring managers were hypothesised to have the opposite traits. These hypotheses were formed on the basis of earlier studies by Burack and Pati (1970a, b), Dubin (1972), McClelland and Winters (1969), Hall (1971) and Kaufman (1974).

Two tests were used in the Jones (1979) study to measure a manager's personality and level of achievement motivation. These were the 16PF (A form) (Cattell *et al*. 1970) and the N-Ach test (Smith 1973). They were administered to three sub-samples of the study population: those who rated themselves the lowest (19) and highest (24) on obsolescence and those in the middle range (22).

ANALYSIS OF RESULTS*

Two statistical tests were used to analyse the results of the 16PF and N-Ach test scores. These were the T-test and discriminant analysis. On classifying the sample into the two groups of high and low obsolescence scoring managers, a test of mean differences was performed for the 17 variables (16PF plus N-Ach). This test was for equality/inequality of the means.

The basic problem was to determine whether or not a difference between the two samples implied a true difference in the parent (managerial) population and if there was a difference, the extent to which it was statistically significant.

The assumptions made were:

1. The data was normal.

2. A test for similar variance was made (F-test). Where the difference was shown to be significant, a pooled variance estimate of T was derived.

Table 3.1 shows the distribution of the 17 variables by means, standard deviations and T-values.

---

* For those not familiar with the statistical techniques, these results are discussed verbally at the end of this chapter (pp. 46—52).

Table 3.1 *Distribution of Personality Variables by Means, Standard Deviations and T-Values*

Variable Name		Mean (*M*)	S.D.	*T*-Value	Significance Level
Factor *A*	Group 1*	5.29	1.88	−1.10	0.277
	Group 2	5.95	1.99		
Factor *B*	Group 1	8.13	1.48	1.98	0.056
	Group 2	7.16	1.68		
Factor *C*	Group 1	5.33	1.86	−2.07	0.045
	Group 2	6.37	1.42		
Factor *E*	Group 1	5.29	1.90	−1.49	0.145
	Group 2	6.21	2.10		
Factor *F*	Group 1	4.88	1.83	−0.13	0.895
	Group 2	4.95	1.75		
Factor *G*	Group 1	6.33	1.83	−0.75	0.495
	Group 2	6.74	1.70		
Factor *H*	Group 1	5.54	1.87	−1.18	0.247
	Group 2	6.32	2.34		
Factor *I*	Group 1	5.46	1.50	−1.07	0.295
	Group 2	6.11	2.28		
Factor *L*	Group 1	4.88	1.78	1.73	0.091
	Group 2	3.95	1.72		

These results indicate that there was a significant difference between the sample means of factors *B* and *C* at the 0.05 level, and there was a significant difference between the sample means of factor *L* and N-Ach at the 0.09 level. These latter two are not considered to be highly significant, although they do show a high degree of difference between the sample means.

This analysis demonstrates that the two population samples differ on three personality variables from the 16PF, and the N-Ach achievement motivation variable. The three persona-

Table 3.1 continued *Distribution of Personality Variables by Means, Standard Deviations and T-Values*

Variable Name		Mean (*M*)	S.D.	*T*-Value	Significance Level
Factor *M*	Group 1	6.46	1.72	0.77	0.448
	Group 2	5.95	2.46		
Factor *N*	Group 1	3.96	1.60	−0.69	0.492
	Group 2	4.32	1.73		
Factor *O*	Group 1	4.92	2.15	0.98	0.333
	Group 2	4.37	1.30		
Factor *Q*1	Group 1	4.79	2.13	−0.64	0.525
	Group 2	5.21	2.12		
Factor *Q*2	Group 1	5.38	1.50	−0.99	0.326
	Group 2	6.00	2.58		
Factor *Q*3	Group 1	5.63	1.66	−0.19	0.804
	Group 2	5.74	2.05		
Factor *Q*4	Group 1	5.13	1.85	−1.03	0.309
	Group 2	4.53	1.93		
N-Ach	Group 1	6.21	1.62	−1.86	0.069
	Group 2	7.05	1.35		

* Group 1 refers to the high obsolescence group
Group 2 refers to the low obsolescence group

lity variables are:

1. Factor *B*   Less intelligent—more intelligent;

2. Factor *C*   Affected by feelings—emotionally stable;

3. Factor *L*   Trusting—suspicious.

The conclusion drawn from these results is that managers who rate themselves highly obsolescent are:

1. More intelligent;

2. Affected by feelings;

3. Suspicious;

4. Have a low need for achievement.

Whereas, managers who rate themselves up-to date (low on obsolescence) are:

1. Less intelligent;

2. Emotionally stable;

3. Trusting;

4. Have a high need for achievement.

The remaining 14 personality variables of 16PF were not found to be significantly different within these two sample groups of managers in as far as the T-test could measure.

Figure 3.1 shows the distribution of 16PF results by the high and low obsolescence scoring sample groups. The graph of these results illustrates the difference between the sample means on each of the 16 variables measured by the 16PF test.

The next stage in the analysis of these results was discriminant analysis.

The decision to use discriminant analysis in this research was based on its ability to determine whether there were any significant differences between high and low obsolescence scoring managers on their 16PF and N-Ach results. The two uses to which it was put were:

1. In the analysis stage — to determine which variables discriminate most powerfully between the high and

Source Traits		A	B	C	E	F	G	H	I	L	M	N	O	Q1	Q2	Q3	Q4
High obsolescence group N = 24 (——)	Mean	5.3	8.1	5.3	5.3	4.9	6.3	5.5	5.5	4.9	6.5	4.0	4.9	4.8	5.4	5.6	5.1
	Standard deviation	1.9	1.5	1.9	1.9	1.8	1.8	1.9	1.5	1.8	1.7	1.6	2.1	2.1	1.5	1.7	1.8
Low obsolescence group N = 19 (----)	Mean	5.9	7.2	6.4	6.2	4.9	6.7	6.3	6.1	3.9	5.9	4.3	4.4	5.2	6.0	5.7	4.5
	Standard deviation	2.0	1.7	1.4	2.1	1.7	1.7	2.3	2.3	1.7	2.5	1.7	1.3	2.1	2.6	2.1	1.9

FIGURE 3.1 Distribution of 16 PF Results by High and Low Obsolescence Samples

* Standard ten point score.

low obsolescence scoring managers using their 16PF and N-Ach results;

2. In the classification stage — to determine how well the function is able to discriminate between the two groups of managers.

Stepwise discriminant analysis was used because the main interest was in the variables used in the discriminant function, rather than in the function itself. This also provided the facility of checking which variables were used in each step. The variables were entered in the order of magnitude of their contribution to the discriminant function. The cut-off point chosen in terms of explanation was based on how much each added variable contributed to the accuracy of the discriminant function. This was at the point where a change in Rao's V ceased to be significant ($P<0.05$). Table 3.2 shows the distribution of the significant variables in the discriminant function.

Of the 17 variables (16PF plus N-Ach) entered in the analysis, only eight contributed significantly to the discriminant function. The most important variables were factors C (Affected by Feelings—Emotionally Stable), B (Less Intelligent—More Intelligent) and L (Trusting—Suspicious). These three were also significant in the results of the T-test, outlined above. Factors E (Humble—Assertive), $Q2$ (Group-Dependent—Self Sufficient), A (Reserved—Outgoing), N (Forthright—Shrewd) and M (Practical—Imaginative) also contributed significantly to the function.

This discriminant function was reasonably accurate in describing the two groups of managers, for Wilk's = 0.4895 ($P = 0.001$) and the canonical correlation was 0.715, which means that 51.12% of the variance in the discriminant function can be explained by the two groups. This means that the discriminant function is a good mathematical description of the differences between the two groups.

The next stage was the classification stage where known

Table 3.2 *Distribution of Significant Variables in the Discriminant Function*

Variables	Rao's V	Change in Rao's V	P
Factor C Affected by feelings—Emotionally stable	4.0	4.0	0.045
Factor B Less Intelligent—More Intelligent	12.4	8.4	0.004
Factor L Trusting—Suspicious	16.0	3.6	0.056
Factor E Humble—Assertive	22.4	6.4	0.011
Factor $Q2$ Group-dependent—Self-sufficient	26.3	3.8	0.050
Factor A Reserved—Outgoing	31.7	5.4	0.020
Factor N Forthright—Shrewd	39.6	7.9	0.005
Factor M Practical—Imaginative	42.8	3.2	0.074

cases were reclassified to determine the extent to which the discriminant function was able to classify or predict in which group a case belonged. These results are shown in Table 3.3.

Over four-fifths (86.05%) of known cases were correctly classified, which is well above the level expected by chance (50%) and is statistically significant ($X^2 = 26.434, P = 0.001$). A higher proportion of the 'High Obsolescence' group were correctly classified (87.5%) than the 'Low Obsolescence' group (84.2%). These results indicate that there are significant differences between the two groups.

Table 3.3 *Prediction Results of Discriminant Analysis using 16PF and N-Ach Variables*

Actual Group	Predicted Group	
	Group 1	Group 2
Group 1 High Obsolescence ($N = 24$)	26 (87.5%)	3 (12.5%)
Group 2 Low Obsolescence ($N = 19$)	3 (15.8%)	16 (84.2%)

DISCUSSION OF RESULTS

The results of these analyses show that the original hypothesis was partly upheld in that the high obsolescence scoring managers were found to be reserved, affected by feelings, humble, suspicious, imaginative, forthright and group-dependent. The results refuted the hypothesis in relation to intelligence, while the remaining eight factors ($F, G, H, I, O, Q1$, $Q3$ and $Q4$) were not found to be significant on T-test analysis. Likewise, they were not found to contribute significantly to the discriminant function and hence could not be used to discriminate between the two groups of managers.

The T-test analysis shows a significant difference between the sample means in relation to the N-Ach variable ($P = 0.06$). However, it did not contribute significantly to the discriminant function. The low obsolescence scoring managers had a significantly higher level of need achievement than the high obsolescence scoring group.

The results of the two types of analyses carried out on the 16PF and N-Ach test score are summarised in Table 3.4. This table includes only those characteristics which were significant to each of the two samples.

These results show distinct differences between the two groups of managers which indicate that managers' personalities influence their susceptibility to obsolescence. The up-to-date managers are more outgoing than the obsolescent

46

Table 3.4 *Summary of Characteristics of Low and High Obsolescence Samples*

Factors	Low Obsolescence Group ($N = 19$)	High Obsolescence Group ($N = 24$)
A	Outgoing	Reserved
B	Less intelligent	More intelligent
C	Emotionally stable	Affected by feelings
E	Assertive	Humble
L	Trusting	Suspicious
M	Practical	Imaginative
N	Shrewd	Forthright
Q2	Self-sufficient	Group-dependent
N-Ach	High motivation to achieve	Low motivation to achieve

ones. That is, they are easy-going, participative and enjoy social recognition. They are more generous in their social relationships, ready to co-operate, adaptable and not afraid of criticism. These characteristics suggest that these managers interact better with peers and thus are helped to keep up-to-date. This finding is corroborated by that of Rosenbloom (1967). Their adaptability also helps them to cope with change and so keep abreast of new developments in their field (McKinnon 1962 and Argyris 1965). Cattell *et al.* (1970) indicate that this trait is characteristic of business executives. The obsolescent managers were more reserved, less adaptable and hence not as capable of responding to change.

Although the obsolescent managers scored slightly higher on intelligence than the up-to-date group, it appears that this alone was not sufficient to ward off obsolescence.

Both groups were well above average in intelligence, however, compared with the general population, although slightly lower than the sample of senior managers at the Adminstrative Staff College, Henley, reported by Hartston and Mottram (1975).

Kaufman (1974) notes that intelligence is an important factor in relation to obsolescence. He states that, 'inadequate cognitive ability is the most important personal characteristic that predisposes an individual to obsolescence'. Why then are the low obsolescence managers in our sample marginally lower in intelligence than the high obsolescence ones? First, the 16PF scale of intelligence is not a very comprehensive or valid measure of intellectual capacity, but rather a crude indicator. Nevertheless, it does show slight differences between the two groups. Second, and the most probable explanation, is that managers as a group show very high intelligence scores in respect to the general population anyway, so we are only differentiating between intelligent and very intelligent managers in our obsolescence groups. Kaufman's (1974) contention may be accurate for other groups of workers, but not for managers and other professionals. It may be that a minimal amount of intelligence is required to inoculate against obsolescence, but given this basic level, the more important contributory factors are attitudes toward learning ability, job challenge, working for organisations that encourage innovation, and a myriad of other individual and work characteristics.

The up-to-date managers were emotionally stable while the obsolescent group were more affected by feelings. Emotional stability suggests that these managers were mature, calm, phlegmatic, realistic about life and able to maintain group morale. Hartston and Mottram (1975) indicate that this variable, 'has less influence on what occupation a man selects or finds himself in, than on his attitude towards his role and general satisfaction with his lot'. Perhaps it is because these managers have a positive perception of their careers and are satisfied with their jobs that they are interested in keeping up-to-date.

The up-to-date group were also found to be more assertive while the obsolescent group were humble. This assertiveness is usually expressed in more self-assurance, independence and dominance.

This finding corroborates those of Kaufman (1974) and Hall (1971) who report that managers who are in control of their situations will have a positive self-concept. Cattell et al. (1970) indicate that managers who score high on this variable show, 'more effective role interaction and democratic procedure. They also show a low but significant correlation with achievement motivation'.

The obsolescent group scored high on suspicion which indicates that they are not very adaptable, neither cheerful nor composed and not such good team workers. This is clearly related to being reserved as outlined above. These traits appear to be uncharacteristic of British managers according to Hartston and Mottram (1975). The up-to-date managers are more trusting which is linked with a positive self-concept in the 16PF secondary factor of adjustment (low anxiety) and so corroborates the findings of Kaufman (1974) and Hall (1971).

The obsolescent group of managers also appear to be the more imaginative which suggests that they are unconventional, egocentric, sensitive, somewhat impractical and undependable. These characteristics appear to indicate that they are unrealistic in their approach to their work and perhaps do not fully appreciate the necessity of keeping up-to-date, or if they do, they are not dependable enough to do something about it.

The obsolescent managers were forthright which suggests that they were gregarious, natural, had simple tastes and were lacking in self-insight. This lack of self-insight may indicate an inability to recognise their own weakness and so not realise the fact that they have become obsolescent.

The up-to-date managers were self-sufficient which is characterised by being independent, resolute, making decisions and taking action. These traits are similar to those mentioned by Hall (1971) in reference to low obsolescent managers. The obsolescent managers were the more group-dependent and hence not as well able to stand on their own feet.

Finally, the up-to-date managers had a high need for achievement which corroborates the findings of McClelland and Winters (1969), Kaufman (1974) and Chambers (1964). High levels of need achievement were found to be associated with entrepreneurial behaviour, innovative risk-taking and business success (McClelland and Winters 1969). Kaufman (1974) reported that a lack of motivation was the most frequently cited factor in an individual becoming out-of-date.

Psychological Interpretation of the Results:

A number of comparisons were made between the results from this study and those supplied in the IPAT Information Bulletin (1963) in order to help interpret the data within an occupational context. Cattell *et al.* (1970) and Tatsuoka and Cattell (1970) both provide further detailed information about the use of the 16PF in occupational settings. In making these comparisons with the IPAT (1963) information, the concepts described in the bulletin are taken as given, and the scores used from this research are composite group scores rather than individual scores.

Mental Health Index:

The first comparison is concerned with mental health. This can be made through a high composite score which is achieved when individual scores are high on factors C and F, and low on O and $Q4$. The range is from 4—40, with a mean of 22. The high obsolescent group scored a mean of 20.2 which is the same as that for the low obsolescent group. This indicates that both groups are similar in terms of mental health, though below the mean indicated in the bulletin. This

50

result indicates both that groups were slightly below average on mental health, but not to the extent of showing signs of pathology.

Ability to Learn:
The IPAT (1963) derived a composite score for 'ability to learn and capacity to grow in a new job'. This seems to be particularly important in terms of managerial obsolescence. It is characterised by high scores in factors B, G and $Q3$, and low score on F. The normative data indicates a mean (M) of 22 (range 4—40). The high obsolescent group scored a mean of 24.9, compared to 24.5 for the low obsolescent group. This result indicates that both groups are above average on this characteristic and in fact the high obsolescent group show a higher ability to learn than the low obsolescent group. This result is somewhat surprising because the high obsolescent group indicate that they have a poor perception of their learning ability, feel that it has deteriorated in recent years and do not enjoy new learning experiences while the opposite is true for the low obsolescent group.

Both groups of managers appear to be above average in ability to learn and to grow in a new job.

Entrepreneurial Traits:
The high obsolescent group scored lower on factor E ($M = 5.3$) compared to the low obsolescent group ($M = 6.2$), thus indicating that they were less assertive, aggressive, stubborn and competitive, all traits traditionally associated with the entrepreneurial manager. Furthermore, the high obsolescent group scored low on factor $Q2$ ($M = 5.4$) compared to the low obsolescent group ($M = 6.0$). This suggests that they are less self-sufficient and resourceful, which are also associated with an entrepreneurial profile. Both of these factors contributed significantly to the discriminant function. The high obsolescent group scored lower on factors H ($M = 5.5$), N ($M = 4.0$) and $Q1$ ($M = 4.8$) which are also uncharacteristic of an entrepreneurial profile.

These results indicate that the high obsolescent group were less entrepreneurial than the low obsolescent group of managers.

In further comparisons, the high obsolescent group were less well-adjusted than the low obsolescent group, in that they scored lower on factors C ($M = 5.3$) and $Q3$ ($M = 5.6$). They were also more reserved (factor A, $M = 5.3$) suspicious (factor L, $M = 4.9$) and imaginative (factor M, $M = 6.5$). The latter of these suggests that the high obsolescent group were the more creative (Stein 1968).

CHAPTER 4

Job Characteristics and Obsolescence

As a result of the expansion of new knowledge and the potential deterioration of previously held expertise, it is apparent that managers and professionals will be vulnerable to obsolescence once their formal professional education/ training is completed. It is after that point that they become dependent on their own *self-education* strategies for updating, which are unlikely to be as systematic or comprehensive as those in the formal setting they have left. Obsolescence, however, does not appear to be equally distributed within an occupational group. Some managers become obsolete more quickly or more severely than others for a variety of reasons, while others become obsolete in some areas and not in others. Previous research with engineers illustrates this point, in that it indicates wide variations in terms of 'felt' obsolescence (Raudsepp 1964b) and in measured obsolescence (Perrucci and Rothman 1969). Their research suggests that education and experience influence vulnerability to obsolescence. For example, engineers with advanced degrees exhibited significantly less obsolescence than those with only a bachelors degree, and obsolescence generally increased with increasing experience, but not in a strict linear progression as might be expected (Perrucci and Rothman 1969).

The nature of the managerial role suggests that at least some of the variation in the process of becoming obsolete might have its genesis in the alternative career paths chosen by individuals. For example, if an individual enters an administrative position it is likely to render him more vulnerable to obsolescence, as he will have less time for updating technical knowledge than if he entered a teaching or research career. This was confirmed by Rothman and Perrucci (1971) who reported that the highest levels of obsolescence were experienced by those in administrative positions, while the lowest were experienced by those in research and development positions. They conclude that obsolescence tends to decrease as the extent of involvement in professional activities increases. They also report that limited technical responsibility increases vulnerability to obsolescence by allowing the degeneration of existing knowledge through disuse, and failing to stimulate self-education because of the minimal expectations requirements of such positions. Role performance, when differentiated in terms of function, also requires different amounts and types of knowledge and expertise. For example, the demands of research and development personnel are qualitatively different from those in production or sales etc.

Norgren and Warner (1966) report that research and development personnel must be conversant with the newest knowledge and skills in their field in order to maintain high performance, while for other activities it may not be as important.

FIRST JOB EXPERIENCE

There is increasing evidence to suggest that a manager's first job is a crucial determinant of later job performance and vulnerability to obsolescence. The most clear-cut support for the importance of *first job experiences* is provided by the

Bell Systems' long-term management progress study (Kaufman 1974). This study found that the challenge and demands experienced during the first year of work by newly-hired college graduates tended to have a greater influence on eventual performance and career success than did the challenge and demands of succeeding years. This involved the degree to which new managers were expected to utilise their knowledge and skills, use new methods, solve novel problems, apply their learning capacity, become involved in self-development, commit their time and energy and demonstrate initiative. On the other hand, managers who have limited work challenge are likely to become frustrated, reduce their aspirations, or perhaps leave the organisation. The results of the Bell Systems' management study are summarised as follows:

1. Of those who voluntarily left the company early in their careers, 55% did so because of unchallenging work;

2. Of those who had been highly challenged by their early work experiences, 70% increased their motivation to achieve, compared with only 8% of those with unchallenging assignments;

3. There was an increase in concern for really accomplishing something, as distinct from advancement or making more money, among those who experienced challenging jobs early in their career, whereas there was a decrease in desire for accomplishment among those who experienced low initial work challenge.

(Kaufman 1974).

Although it has been demonstrated that 'first jobs' play a major part in a manager's future career, it does pose a dilemma for organisations because they are very often reluctant to assign a difficult job to a newly-recruited manager for fear of failure. This could have serious consequences both for the organisation and the individual manager. Much of this reluctance is also based on the inexperience of the new recruit, yet unless he is given some realistic assignments he will continue to remain inexperienced. Perhaps this is related

COMBATING MANAGERIAL OBSOLESCENCE

in some ways to the developmental stages of child development as identified by Piaget (1953), where there is a distinct
series of stages that a child goes through from birth to
maturity. During the process of maturation, there is no point
in trying to teach certain cognitive or motor skills unless
the child has reached a stage of development capable of
comprehending them. In the case of management, it is often
felt that there is no point in giving managers certain tasks
until they have reached a level of 'maturity' which would
allow them to carry them out effectively. Dalton *et al.* (1977)
suggest that the job assignment is the single most important
variable in career development and there are many ways in
which it can be manipulated. A person who is seen as too
narrow can be moved to a new project that forces him to
apply his existing skills to new problems. Although a change
in job assignment is not in itself a panacea, it can be a major
stimulant in helping people develop their careers.

Some difficulties faced by new recruits are that their
skills and abilities are not being used, they do not know
how to create challenge in their jobs and they are often
perceived as a threat to superiors (Hall 1971). Newly-
recruited managers often possess high levels of skills and
abilities, having recently completed advanced educational
and other training. They are usually fully aware of up-to-date
techniques and anxious to apply them in their new jobs.
The organisation, on the other hand, has established procedures for doing things and tends to resist innovation. The
young manager has often got false aspirations as to his
abilities, and when he comes in contact with his superiors
he feels that they are behind the times and incompetent
because they do not recognise his 'worth'. Because he often
does not know how to create his own challenges, he must
rely on his superiors and the organisation to give them to
him. When they are not forthcoming, he gets frustrated.
This reliance on others is due to the fact that he is accus-
tomed to being given challenging projects in school or university and not creating them for himself. Indeed, research has

shown that people tend to be rather passive about even major career decisions, the type of organisation they work for, whether or not to change jobs, and the type of jobs they should accept (Roe and Burach 1967).

FRUSTRATIONS OF OLDER MANAGERS

New managers often threaten their superiors by their advanced knowledge and this is probably a major contributor to the syndrome of *unused potential* (Schein 1968). Another aspect of this threat is the fact that the superior may be in a terminal position, or frustrated in his attempts to keep up-to-date, and is now confronted with this 'whiz kid' who is full of ideas and anxious to impress everyone and leave his mark. A further problem arises because of the high starting salaries available to new recruits. These are generally much higher today than they were when the superior first began his career and this can be an additional source of resentment. From a more positive point of view, there is evidence to suggest that if the superior is in a secure position and not far from retirement (hence with little to lose), he may take the new recruit under his wing and act as a mentor to help him adjust to the organisation (Dalton *et al.* 1977). Unless this positive approach is taken by the superior the young manager may change in his self-image, attitudes, aspirations and motivation in a negative direction. He may become less optimistic about succeeding within the organisation (Campbell 1967). He may see himself as having less impact on the organisation, and so his values may tend to conform to those of the organisation (Schein 1967). These changes can increase the manager's vulnerability to obsolescence in the long term.

At more advanced stages in managers' careers, it is important that they continue to have challenging work, otherwise they too will become frustrated and prone to obsolescence. Later comments will be made on the mis-utilisation and under-utilisation of managers. These have

57

consequences for maintaining up-to-date knowledge and skills. Research by Raudsepp (1964a), Ritti (1971b), Kornhauser (1962) and Hirch (1958) all indicate negative outcomes from under-utilisation of managers' ability. It leads to loss of job satisfaction, frustration with the amount of time spent on administrative details that could be handled by less qualified people, and a lack of motivation to keep up-to-date. In order to overcome some of these difficulties, superiors should take greater care in allocating job assignments. This can be done by management attempting to understand better the career behaviour patterns of subordinates, the organisational work, and other characteristics that influence individual career decisions. This may require special performance appraisal procedures, changes in reporting styles, discussion seminars, etc. Resulting from these, management actions can be planned so as to be responsive to the requirements of each situation, and attuned to individual career planning behaviour, and steps can be taken to improve the communication of management's concern for effective individual career planning in line with organisational goals (Walker 1973). The creation of semi-annual work planning and review programmes can also be helpful in maintaining and effectively utilising the skills and abilities of managers (McGregor 1960).

TECHNOLOGICAL CHANGE

A major factor affecting managers' ability to keep abreast of new developments is the rapid technological changes occurring in industry at all levels. In his article on 'personal obsolescence', Fox (1965) identified automation and cybernetics as two factors most instrumental in causing technological change. These factors have become even more evident in recent times with the move towards capital-intensive industries, resulting in higher rates of unemployment and redundancies at both management and other levels (Hartley 1978 and Jones 1979). Three fears associated with these technological changes are:

1. That automation and cybernetics will do away with many jobs and so swell the numbers of the unemployed;

2. The computer will become so intelligent that it will replace man; and

3. That many cannot adapt themselves to the radical changes happening at an ever-increasing rate in technology.

(Fox 1965).

These fears and their consequences are enumerated in Toffler's (1970) book, *Future Shock*, which describes the variety and rapidity of changes both technological and otherwise which people face today, and the problems of adjustment brought about by these changes. The extent of obsolescence is affected not only by the rate of technical change, but also by the relative state of technological refinement or degree of automation (Crossman 1960). This is evidenced in Marn and Heffernan's (1960) study of power plants where it was found that:

. . . 97% of the employees reported that their jobs required more training now than earlier, . . . jobs were perceived by the men to be ones with increased responsibility requiring greater degrees and amounts of training than did their older jobs.

At the management level, Barrett *et al.* (1971) indicated a clear awareness by personnel of the need for their own educational upgrading: 'a large majority — between 70% and 85% — expected demands on their reading, writing and speaking skills to increase greatly in the next five years. Moreover, over 80% of the respondents expressed their realisation, in terms of both preferences and expectations, that they will require to increase knowledge in their own fields of specialisation'. The National Science Foundation (1969) report made similar comments in reference to scientists and engineers.

The impact of computer technology is directly felt by

middle managers in particular. This is because they work directly with the computer and use computer information frequently to analyse and identify problem areas, in addition to evaluating alternative courses of action which might be used by their superiors (Brady 1967). Further problems faced by managers which can lead to obsolescence are: when an expert is used over and over again in a narrow specialism, thus giving no scope to develop or expand his knowledge or skills; job pressures can 'burn out' an employee in his productive years, with little time allowed for refurbishment and growth until it is too late; work priorities can interfere with the employees' educational commitments; and lastly, employees may become over-committed to the job or organisation at the expense of family life and outside interests, thus leading to a narrowing view of life and work which can often 'blind' them to the need for change or updating in their careers (Miller 1972).

RESEARCH FINDINGS

In our study, the following variables were examined in relation to managerial obsolescence (see Figure 4.1):

Management function;
Level in hierarchy;
Decision-making responsibilities; and
Challenge of job (see questionnaire in Appendix 1).

Each of these will be commented on here in terms of the study findings. For detailed statistical information on the relationship between these variables and different aspects of obsolescence, see Appendix 2.

Management Function:
Management function was found to be significantly related to managerial obsolescence. The most up-to-date managers were those in Finance, followed by Personnel, Production

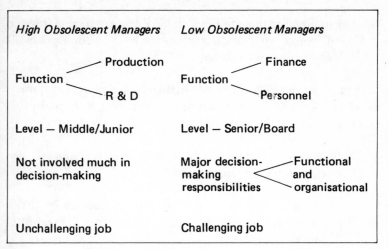

FIGURE 4.1 *Job Characteristics and Obsolescence*

and R & D. The following explanations for these results were proposed by managers during discussions of the results with them. A total of 65 managers were involved in these interviews. The explanations were as follows:

1. Financial managers tend to study longer into their careers than other managers;

2. They are more likely to belong to professional associations and the associations they do belong to tend to provide a better service for their members than other associations;

3. When one looks at the daily papers there are always many pages dealing specifically with finance (e.g. Financial Times), while there is little written on a daily basis about other aspects of management;

4. What goes on, or happens in a company, ultimately costs money and so the financial managers will be aware of it;

5. Financial managers tend to have the greatest influence on company policy and must be in touch with all aspects of the company.

Personnel managers rated themselves the second most up-to-date group. Some reasons put forward to explain this were:

1. Personnel managers often have degrees and so are better educated then many others;

2. They tend to study well into their careers in order to become members of the Institute of Personnel Management;

3. They often hold responsibility for training and so are aware of the importance of continuing education/ training and what is available in the way of courses, seminars, conferences etc.;

4. They have a need to keep in touch with all aspects of their companies because of recruitment and industrial relations requirements.

Production managers rated themselves second highest on obsolescence. The reasons put forward by managers to explain this were:

1. Production managers generally come from poor educational backgrounds, having left school early to take up appenticeships;

2. The lack of formal education tends to make them shy away from formal learning situations because they have a poor perception of their learning ability;

3. They are generally well skilled in handling machinery and do not feel the need to attend training courses;

4. They are often unaware of new techniques such as production scheduling and control, materials handling and streamlining production processes;

5. There are not many courses available for production managers, and those that are, tend to be too general;

6. They are not likely to belong to professional associations;

7. Their work tends to be mainly routine.

R & D managers rated themselves the most obsolete of all four functions. The reasons given to explain this were:

1. R & D managers are aware of the volume of literature and material published each year in their particular field of interest. However, since they cannot possibly hope to read it all, they conclude that they must be missing out on important developments. This may not be necessarily true, but they often do not realise it;

2. Because they cannot read everything, they feel that their knowledge is out-of-date;

3. They often tend to specialise in very narrow fields of interest and thus lose touch with other areas within their disciplines;

4. They generally take a long time doing a narrow piece of research which allows them little time to devote to other matters:

5. They have a tendency to remain isolated from other areas of their companies and not become involved much in policy matters.

Level in hierarchy:

The results of our study show that the hierarchical level of managers was significantly related to only one aspect of obsolescence. The results indicated that the more senior the managers, the more up-to-date they rated themselves. Perhaps the reason for this lies in the fact that the more senior the managers, the more challenging they found their jobs. The more senior they were, the more important their decisions in relation to both their functions and their companies. In addition to this, they were also older, more likely to be qualified in finance, have the most management experience, and to have worked outside of the country and at a management level. All these factors when taken together seem to be quite important, whereas individually they may not be so. Dalton *et al.* (1977) indicate that as a manager gets older he tends to be more willing to take risks and is less concerned with security, particularly as he gets closer to retirement. The finding that older senior managers were less obsolete than younger junior/middle ones has important implications for the future of their companies. If young junior/middle managers feel that they are obsolete then the consequences of this for their own careers as well as for their organisations are serious. This is especially so, since they are the ones who are in direct contact with technological changes, as discussed above. Whether in fact they are the most obsolete is difficult to say, but if they are, then there is a great need to tackle obsolescence at this level. The answer may lie in the fact that junior and middle managers may be under-utilised in terms of their ability. This has been found to be an important factor de-motivating managers to keep up-to-date (Raudsepp 1964a, Ritti 1971b, Kornhauser 1962 and Hirch 1958). This is because under-utilisation leads to loss of job satisfaction, frustration and lack of motivation to update, which reinforces the argument that senior managers should be aware of the importance of assigning challenging jobs to their subordinates (Kaufman 1974).

Decision-making responsibilities:

Functional decision-making was found to be significantly related to most aspects of obsolescence, while company decision-making was significantly related to all obsolescence variables. These results corroborate the findings of Raudsepp (1964a), and Kaufman (1974), both of whom indicate that decision-making responsibilities were important in relation to career challenge and hence influenced managerial obsolescence. If managers make important contributions to their companies, then they are more likely to be listened to and so influence the future of their companies. This in turn will probably have the effect of giving them greater job satisfaction and lead to the realisation of higher order personal needs such as enhanced self-esteem and possibly self-actualisation (Maslow 1943). If, on the other hand, they are not listened to, they are unlikely to contribute as much to their company, become dissatisfied, and hence vulnerable to obsolescence.

Challenge of job:

Challenge of job was also found to be significantly related to most aspects of obsolescence. The related variable of, 'the extent to which managers' jobs utilised their professional skills and abilities', was likewise significantly related to obsolescence. These results are consistent with the findings of Raudsepp (1964a), Ritti (1971b) and Kaufman (1974), all of whom indicate that job challenge is a major factor in keeping managers up-to-date. The mis-utilisation or under-utilisation of managers was found to result in frustration and dissatisfaction (Kaufman 1974).

SUMMARY

These findings emphasise the crucial importance of job or career influences on managerial obsolescence. It appears that obsolescence affects different functions to a greater or lesser degree. This is further influenced by the hierarchical level of the manager, with those at senior level being less prone than those at middle or junior levels. Managers' decision-making responsibilities and challenge of their jobs are additional factors which greatly affect their potential or actual obsolescence ratings. It seems that the greater the influence managers have on their companies and the more challenge they get from their jobs, the less likely they will experience obsolescence.

CHAPTER 5

Influence of Boss and Colleagues on Obsolescence Behaviour

RELATIONSHIPS AT WORK

An important factor influencing managers at work has to do with the nature of their relationships with their boss, subordinates and colleagues. A number of behaviourial scientists (Argyris 1964 and Cooper 1973) have suggested that good relationships between members of a work group are a central factor in individual and organisational health and development. Nevertheless, very little research work has been done in this area to either support or reject this hypothesis. French and Caplan (1973) define poor relations as 'those which include low trust, low supportiveness and low interest in listening to and trying to deal with problems that confront the organisational member'. Some notable studies in this area are by Kahn *et al.* (1964), French and Caplan (1970) and Buck (1972). Both the Kahn *et al.* and French and Caplan studies came to roughly the same conclusion, that mistrust of persons one worked with was positively related to high ambiguity which led to inadequate communications between people and to 'psychological strain in the form of low job satisfaction and to feelings of job-related threat to one's well-being'. However, in the Kahn *et al.* study, poor relations with one's subordinates was significantly associated with feelings of threat from colleagues and superiors, but not associated with threat from subordinates.

Buck (1972) on the other hand focused on the attitude and relationship of workers and managers to their immediate boss using Fleishman's leadership questionnaire on consideration and initiating structure. The consideration factor was associated with behaviour indicative of friendship, mutual trust, respect and a certain warmth between boss and subordinate. He found that those workers who felt that their boss was low on 'consideration' reported feeling more job pressure. Workers who were under pressure reported that their bosses did not give them criticism in a helpful way, played favourites with subordinates, 'pulled rank' and took advantage of them whenever they got a chance. Buck concludes that the 'considerate behaviour of supervisors appears to have contributed significantly (inversely) to feelings of job pressure'.

Officially, one of the most critical functions of a manager is his supervision of other people's work. It has long been accepted that an 'inability to delegate' might be a problem, but now a new potential source of stress is being introduced in the manager's interpersonal skills — he must learn to 'manage by participation'. Donaldson and Gowler (1975) point to the factors which may make today's zealous emphasis on participation a cause of resentment, anxiety and stress for the manager concerned:

1. mismatch of formal and actual power

2. the manager may well resent the erosion of his formal role and authority (and the loss of status and rewards)

3. he may be subject to irreconcilable pressure — e.g. to

be both participative and to achieve high production, and

4. his subordinates may refuse to participate.

Particularly for those with technical and scientific backgrounds (a 'things-orientation'), relationships can be a low priority (seen as 'trivial', 'petty', time-consuming and an impediment to doing the job well) and one would expect their interactions to be more a source of stress than those of 'people-oriented' managers.

Besides the obvious factors of office politics and colleague rivalry, we find another element of how stress can be caused not only by the pressure of relationships but also by its opposite — lack of adequate social support in difficult situations (Lazarus 1966). At highly competitive managerial levels it is likely that problem-sharing will be inhibited for fear of appearing weak; and much of the (American) literature particularly mentions the isolated life of the top executive as an added source of strain.

Morris (1975) encompasses this whole area of relationships in one model — what he calls the 'cross of relationships' (see Figure 5.1).

Whilst he acknowledges the differences between relation-

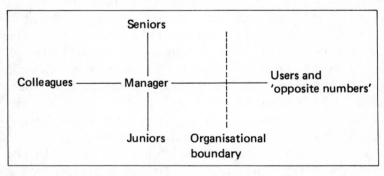

FIGURE 5.1 *The Cross of Relationships*

ships on the various continua, he feels that the focal manager must bring all four into 'dynamic balance' in order to be able to deal with the stress of his position. Morris' suggestion seems 'only sensible' when we realise that the manager spends a high proportion of his work time with other people. In a research programme to find out exactly what managers do, Minzberg (1973) showed just how much time is spent in interaction. In an intensive study of a small sample of chief executives, he found that in a large organisation a mere 22% of time was spent in desk work sessions, the rest being taken by telephone calls (6%), scheduled meetings (59%), unscheduled meetings (10%) and other activities (3%). In small organisations basic desk work played a larger part (52%), but nearly 40% was still devoted to face-to-face contacts of one kind or another.

According to Dubin (1972a), one of the chief situational determinants for motivating managers to update themselves is the behaviour of their supervisors. Supervisors were not found to be assisting their subordinates' growth and development in a study of engineers carried out by Dubin and Marlow (1965) and of managers by Dubin, Alderman and Marlow (1967). Almost two-thirds of 2,090 professional engineers reported that their supervisors took a non-commital attitude towards their further education and development. Similarly, 51% of 3,600 managers reported the same attitudes on the part of their superiors. These findings were corroborated in a study carried out by the US National Science Foundation (1969), which found that about one-third of the scientists and almost a half of the engineers interviewed, reported attitudes of non-interest on the part of their superiors. In another study, Landis (1969) asked managers 'How does your immediate supervisor feel about further job-directed education or training?'. Fifteen per cent reported 'very encouraging'; 47% 'somewhat encouraging'; and 37% 'not encouraging at all'. He thus concluded that it is:

the immediate supervisor that counts in the development of sub-ordinates. If a boss does not encourage a man, he will not take further course work . . . unless the supervisor is willing to encourage and accommodate his men in spite of the possible interference with his work schedule, few men will undertake continuing studies.

Locke (1970) concludes that the supervisor aids in the motivational process by helping the subordinate to specify his goals within the context of his job and ensuring that the facilities exist for the subordinate to update his skills and to realise his goals. This takes the supervisor out of his traditional 'regulator role' and into that of developer and facilitator of subordinates' motivational potential.

The National Science Foundation (1969) provides further evidence of the key position occupied by the supervisor. Three types of supervisor were identified: the *innovator*, the *administrator* and the *inactive supervisor*. The innovator:

tries to create new opportunities in addition to existing ones, to provide novel and interesting ways for subordinates to undertake continuing education. The administrator conceives of his job as implementing organisation policies and encouraging subordinates to use existing resources for self-development. The inactive super-visor is passive and non-commital in his attitudes. He conceives self-development as a responsibility of the employee apart from the working environment. He neither stimulates subordinates to pursue additional knowledge nor initiates continuing education on their behalf.

A further role that supervisors could play is that of coach. This entails telling the subordinates what they should know and what is expected of them, and the results they are expected to achieve. They are then given tasks to help their development, and feedback is provided to ensure that they know how they are doing. They should be given guidance and assistance when needed, and rewarded or penalised on the basis of results. Hinrichs (1966) describes this type of coaching as a direct expression of two basic employee development principles: '(1) most employee development occurs on the job, and (2) personnel development must be a line-management responsibility'.

These studies all emphasise that in any programme to alleviate obsolescence, the supervisor has a major role to play. This is because he acts as the link between the organisation and the individual employee, and so can translate organisational policy into meaningful action, yet retaining the personal touch. This is important in order to motivate employees to engage in career development programmes to combat or stave off the onset of obsolescence.

The results of our study show that superiors' interest in subordinates' growth and development as professionals was significantly related to managerial obsolescence. Managers from Printing and Paper companies for example indicated that their superiors were most likely to reward high management performance. Managers from Engineering companies, on the other hand, indicated that their superiors were least likely to be interested in their subordinates' development and yet these managers were given the greatest encouragement to innovate.

According to Dubin (1972), one of the chief determinants for motivating managers to update was the influence of superiors. Most studies to date indicate that superiors are not good at encouraging their subordinates to update (Dubin and Marlow 1965, Landis 1969). Landis (1969) suggests that unless a manager is willing to encourage and accommodate the development of his subordinates, few will undertake continuing studies. Locke (1970) indicates that managers can help subordinates to specify their goals in terms of their jobs and secondly, ensure that facilities exist for them to update their knowledge and skills to achieve these goals. The results of this study show that in all three industrial sectors, managers were most likely to classify their superiors as 'administrators' (NSF 1969).

In terms of obsolescence rating, it was found that those who were least obsolete classified their superiors as either 'innovators' or 'inactive supervisors' (NSF 1969).

These results suggest that it is very much up to the individual manager to look after his own updating and, in fact, the low obsolescent manager is one who does this irrespective of any assistance from his supervisor or indeed any help from his/her organisation. Although many writers comment on the importance of the supervisor, and talk about the theoretical role he plays in coaching his subordinates (Hinrichs 1966 and Dalton *et al.* 1977), the most important factor is how management view themselves and take responsibility for their own updating (Mant 1969). Miller (1972) puts it a different way. 'The emphasis by management on the importance of personal growth and human vitality seems to result more from what management does than what management says.'

CHAPTER 6

Organisational Structure and Climate and Managerial Obsolescence

ORGANISATIONAL CLIMATE

A major environmental factor influencing managerial obsolescence is organisational climate. This can be defined as 'organisational and management practices that influence motivation, condition attitudes, and shape behaviour on the part of its members' (House and Rizzo 1971). In reference to this, Dubin (1972) notes that some professionals are made obsolete by the organisation in which they work. They are kept obsolete by unstimulating work and by the limited demands and rigid controls that prevent them from enlarging the scope of their work. Hesseling (1971) states that '. . . organisations must create a challenging environment for inquisitive and speculative members who feel themselves deeply rooted in the organisational reality'. The importance of a suitable organisational climate is essential if it is to provide the kind of work environment conducive to keeping managers up-to-date and preventing the onrush of obsolescence. The characteristics of such a climate are as follows:

74

1. *Achievement* — a desire of the group to do a good contribute to the performance of the company.

2. *Concern for Excellence* — degree to which the grou cerned with improving individual performance, being flexible, innovate and competent;

3. *Problem-Solving Emphasis* — extent to which group anticipates and solves problems related to group functioning;

4. *Reputation* — organisation reflects status and reputation of individuals' work group compared to other work groups;

5. *Training Opportunities* — degree to which the organisation provides training for individuals;

6. *Atmosphere* — degree to which supervisors generate a supportive and friendly atmosphere;

7. *Initial Job Orientation* — individuals are informed of what to expect when they first start on the job.

(Campbell and Beatty, 1971)

ADAPTIVE AND NON-ADAPTIVE ORGANISATIONS

In a similar way, Margulies and Raia (1967) argue that an *adaptive* organisation is the most conducive to individual professional growth. 'The adaptive organisation is one which is flexible and resilient as it responds to feedback from that environment'. Such an organisation is experimental and 'free to change', without rigid conformity to traditional patterns of operation. When being experimental is rewarded, and failure actually becomes part of the learning process, then the organisation is innovative, i.e. more creative in response to tasks. Too often, however, organisational objectives become paramount, so all-pervading that individuals are lost and absorbed in a maze of procedures and rules. Nurturance, on the other hand, reflects the concern of the organisation for the professional growth and development of each individual. When the organisational climate can be described as *open* and the emergent character has a high degree of experimentalism, innovativeness and nurturance, the result is a

75

'healthy' and highly creative organisation — one in which individual motivation and, hence, individual activities contribute to the effective and efficient accomplishment of organisational objectives.

In contrast, the 'non-adaptive organisation is insensitive to its environment and because of rigid conformity to traditional patterns of operations, as well as the existence of many organisational constraints and restrictions, it is inflexible and unchanging'. Since the climate discourages experimentation, the risk of failure is prohibitive. Thus, the concern of the organisation is focused on its task or mission, rather than on the need for individual growth and development. It is 'unhealthy' in that there is a low degree of experimentalism, innovativeness, and nurturance in the climate. Consequently, individual motivation and creativity are suppressed and the result is something less than the accomplishment of total organisational objectives.

From an individual manager's standpoint, he wants more than security and money nowadays, he wants job satisfaction. He wants the opportunity for growth in his career; to be able to learn from experience and expand his knowledge and skills. Managers to-day have career questions they want answered and without these answers, frustration sets in, which leads to morale problems and low productivity (Wool 1973, Blood and Hulin 1967). The response of some managers to this is to resign and change jobs and hence, mobility is used as a vehicle for updating (Mant 1969). This in turn leads to a demand for effective career development and career planning programmes (Hanson 1977).

MIS-UTILISATION & UNDER-UTILISATION

Two major cause of managerial job dissatisfaction are what Kaufman (1974) calls 'mis-utilisation' and 'under-utilisation'. Mis-utilisation is greatest when managers experience light intellectual demands in their jobs together with heavy time pressures. It results from managers working under time pressure at assignments so routine that they could and should be done by clerical personnel. This is confirmed by Ritti (1971a) when he states that the two most important causes of obsolescence among professionals are:

work assignments that do not require knowledge of the latest developments; and

the pressure of schedule demands that leave no time or energy for study.

Data obtained from two independent engineering development laboratories indicate that three out of four of those who report considerable *mis-utilisation* in their work have a problem keeping up-to-date with new developments. On the other hand, over half of those who feel that mis-utilisation is not a problem report having no trouble keeping up-to-date. In essence, managers can avoid obsolescence to the extent that they are required to use their knowledge and skills.

Under-utilisation is similar to mis-utilisation in that it involves only light intellectual demands on the job, but the under-utilised manager has light rather than heavy time demands. This tends to occur frequently at the outset of a manager's career. It is a great danger to the new employee's development, for it results in little job challenge. These problems of utilisation are expected to increase in the future, in that manpower projections show that the rapid growth in the numbers of college-educated workers will force an increasing percentage of them into jobs that do not utilise their ability, knowledge and skills. This is often called 'over-recruiting' and is especially evident in times when there are few jobs, but many highly qualified unemployed workers available to do them.

TOP-HEAVY ORGANISATION

A further cause of obsolescence occurs in what Reeser (1977) calls 'top-heavy organisations'. This is the tendency for managerial levels to become inflated in times of prosperity. He cites an example of this in the aerospace industry in the 1960s, when managerial jobs were created with little objective determination of their need, and managers were hired and promoted with little investigation of their qualifications. Then, as contracts decreased and funds became scarcer, thousands of managers became surplus to the needs of the organisations. This resulted in mass lay-offs of managers in the 1970s. Organisations also took this opportunity to ferret out and terminate employment of those managers whom they felt had become obsolete. An unfortunate offshoot of this was the fact that many of these were middle-aged or older, and the resultant effect on their lives was often traumatic (Chamberlain 1974, and Einstein 1972). Drucker (1971) maintains that corporations are unrealistically adding 'layers of vice presidents', and that there is too much emphasis on building and maintaining hierarchical systems. Moreover, he finds that corporations are overstaffing with young, educated employees, and providing plenty of promotion steps for their early careers. However, these opportunities become severely limited at some midpoint on the ladder, with the result that many individuals in their 30's become stranded in bureaucracies, and the inevitable stagnation leads ultimately to obsolescence.

An ironic aspect of this is that some managers can avoid detection by 'building empires', thus deluding their superiors into thinking they are performing a worthwhile service. Eventually, however, these empires spawn their own obsolescence and, inevitably, managers who are not contributing to the development of the organisation will become costly liabilities (Penzer 1973).

The tendency of many organisations to have a pyramidal model of management hierarchy also leads to obsolescence. This is illustrated in most organisation charts where the numbers of managers decrease as one rises to the top, so that at each successive level there are many competing for fewer jobs. Authority, status and pay all increase as the manager moves up the chart. Implicit in this model is the concept that career development consists of moving as rapidly and as far up the pyramid as possible. This is all in order, as long as upward movement continues. However, the reality of the situation is that at each succeeding level, managers get blocked, in that they cannot progress any further due to competition from colleagues who may be more competent. When a manager realises his dilemma he may decide to relax and take things easy — thus becoming a sure candidate for obsolescence, or he may decide to change direction in his career and try to progress up an alternative route, should one exist, or lastly he may decide to change jobs with the hope of success in another organisation. This latter choice becomes more difficult the older the manager gets and the higher his level of accomplishment. If he has got to a senior management position in company A he may find it difficult to move to a similar position in company B due, for example, to company B's policy of promotion from within. On the other hand, if he is willing to move to a smaller company C he may be fortunate and take over the chief executive position. One way in which organisations have tried to cope with this pyramidal problem is to create a dual ladder for promotion. This allows those with technical expertise to move up a parallel ladder to those in management, without necessarily taking on major management responsibilities. It also provides the organisation with a means of recognising and rewarding the technical contributions of its scientists and engineers. However well this idea looks in theory, it often fails to work in practice. Professional employees begin complaining that: 'ours isn't a real dual ladder; it's been bastardised', 'the men in the upper technical slots don't do real technical work. They prepare proposals and brochures', and 'the real rewards don't go to those on the technical ladder' (Dalton et al. 1977 and Ritti 1971 a, b).

CAREER DEVELOPMENT

Arising from research carried out by Dalton *et al.* (1977), a new model of careers was proposed which can help to overcome obsolescence. This involves *four stages of progress in career development*: the apprenticeship; the journeyman; the mentor and the senior professional. This model was developed for scientists, engineers, accountants and university professors. The four stages are described thus:

Stage 1 – Apprenticeship

Works under the supervision and direction of a more senior professional in the field.

Work is never entirely his own, but is given assignments which are a portion of a larger project or activity being overseen by senior professionals.

Lacks experience and status in organisation.

Is expected willingly to accept supervision and directions.

Is expected to do most of the detailed and routine work on a project.

Is expected to exercise 'directed' creativity and initiative.

Learns to perform well under pressure and accomplish a task within the time budgeted.

Stage II – Journeyman

Goes into depth in one problem or technical area.

Assumes responsibility for a definable portion of the project process or clients.

Works independently and produces significant results.

Develops creativity and a reputation.

Relies less on supervisor or mentor for answers, develops more of his/her own resources to solve problems.

Increases in confidence and ability.

Stage III — Mentor

Involved enough in his/her own work to make significant technical contributions, but begins working in more than one area.

Greater breadth of technical skills and application of those skills.

Stimulates others through ideas and information.

Involved in developing people in one or more of the following ways:

    a. acts as an ideas person for a small group

    b. serves as a mentor to younger professionals

    c. assumes a formal supervisory position.

Deals with the outside to benefit others in organisation, i.e. working out relationships with client organisations, developing new business, etc.

Stage IV — Senior Professional

Influences future direction of organisation through:

    a. original ideas, leading the organisation into new areas of work

    b. organisational leadership and policy formation

    c. integrating the work of others to a significant end.

Influence gained on the basis of:

    a. past ability to assess environmental trends

    b. ability to deal with outside effectively

    c. ability to affect others inside the organisation

Has ability to engage in wide and varied interactions:

    a. at all levels of the organisation

    b. with individuals and groups of future key people.

According to Hanson (1977), these four stages can be correlated with Erik Erikson's theory of adult development which has three stages: intimacy, generativity and ego integration (Gould 1975). The intimacy stage resembles the apprenticeship stage of close contact and supervision. The journeyman stage is like a transitory phase in Erikson's generativity stage which is reflected in the career stage of mentor, where the individual stimulates others through ideas and information and serves as a mentor for young professionals. The senior professional stage is like the ego integration stage in that it is where the professional (adult) meets the final challenges involving both creativity and integration. Both theories require mastery at one stage before progressing successfully to the next. Dalton *et al.* (1977) point out that their model of career stages provides a useful vehicle for describing what Schein (1968) calls the 'organisational definition' of a career — 'the set of expectations held by individuals inside the organisation which guide their decisions about who to move, when, how, and at what speed'. They also indicate that the model has both pragmatic and theoretical implications for those who live in organisations, as well as for those who manage them. Managers need a framework for examining their career decisions and the possible long-term consequences of them. Some managers have found it useful when examining their career development needs to identify the factors that block or facilitate movement between stages. Interruptions in these movements for whatever reason can render the manager susceptible to obsolescence due to lack of incentives, satisfaction or challenge in his job assignments. The indirect costs of this to the organisation are:

providing inadequate support to supervisors;

providing additional work for peers and subordinates who must pick up the slack and frequently work around the obsolescent manager; and

blocking subordinates from promotional opportunities and providing inadequate training and development inputs to subordinates.
(Burack and Pati 1970a)

Another aspect of obsolescence is that affected by

82

organisations' bureaucratic systems, and mis-management by top executives (Berkwitt 1972 and Tarnowieski 1973). Some of these include:

1. 'Lack of candid communication about how they are doing' (Meyer 1974). What this means for the manager is that he needs feedback on how he is doing and why he has been passed over for promotion. This information is essential if the manager hopes to change, for without it his perceived weaknesses will go unchecked, thus leading to obsolescence. Early warning is necessary to ensure that the manager can change before it is too late;

2. 'Fast track' early programmes. This occurs where organisations recruit gifted young people and move them up the ladder rapidly in their early careers only to stop them midway with the inevitable shrinking of promotion opportunities from the middle to the top of the organisation structure. A harsh weeding-out then occurs for the 'not so young' early managerial 'stars' and many are left stranded in positions a long way from the top;

3. Overstaffing is another problem, for it results in the 'survival of the fittest' but again leaves a lot of good talent floundering about at lower levels with no hope of progress. Again a good receipe for obsolescence;

4. Subjective, biased appraisal systems can cause problems for many managers, for if an individual is passed over once (possibly due to a biased appraisal), he has little chance of subsequent promotion;

5. Inequitable development programmes can arise when management development programmes are reserved for the 'bright stars' of the organisation who are on

the way up. The unfortunate side-effect of this is that those who are stuck in the system may require development most, but are least likely to get it, while those who are mobile will get plenty of development, irrespective of need;

6. If a manager refuses promotion for any reason, however legitimate, such as unwillingness to take a transfer, or liking the job he is in, this can often be equated with being unsuccessful. Hence he is left there and not given a second chance to move when perhaps he is more prepared to do so at a later date;

7. Overspecialisation is another problem faced by managers. They are encouraged to specialise and develop narrowly defined skills for particular jobs. This is all very good until these jobs are no longer important to the organisation and the manager is judged as obsolescent. Closely related to this is when technological changes occur which render existing skills obsolete.

WHERE COMPANIES FAIL

The results of these foregoing problems is that middle managers are leaving big business for other fields (Berkwitt 1972). They are revolting against the frustrations of corporate life as suggested by recent industrial research and the business press (Tarnowieski 1973). As Tarnowieski (1973) states, 'while companies worry about phlegmatic employees afflicted with ennui who "retire on company time at full pay", most people are bored to the marrow with their jobs'. Managers are enticed away from their jobs 'for enhanced occupational status and authority'. It is as if they are conscious of the threat of obsolescence and hope to delay or prevent its onrush by means of mobility. This is corroborated by Burack

and Pati (1970 a, b) who list the following company characteristics that lead managers either into obsolescence if they
stay, or else force them to leave altogether:

1. Lack of communication between personnel, manpower planners
   and initiators of technological change;

2. Failure to detect change;

3. Lack of adequate training facilities;

4. Defensive attitude in the absence of know-how;

5. Lack of knowledge about the future manpower requirements;
   and

6. Failure to motivate and encourage individuals to learn for the
   future. Emphasis is on the day-to-day better performance on
   the job, rather than on long-term career development.

TECHNOLOGICAL CHANGE

Although work environments that are affected by change
might be expected to have the greatest problems in dealing
with obsolescence, they actually tend to produce the lowest
numbers of obsolescent managers (Rothman & Perrucci
1970). It has been demonstrated that professionals who are
employed in industries characterised by rapid technological
change acquire a greater amount of new knowledge than do
those who work in less dynamic environments. The incidence
of obsolescence is also less for managers in companies that
experience a high growth rate. These results can be explained
by looking at the challenge created by the work environment.
In other words, managers employed in rapidly-changing
industries such as those engaged in electronics and computers
are stimulated (albeit, forced, if they wish to survive) to
keep up-to-date. On the opposite front, managers who are
employed in slow-changing organisations such as car manufacturing may become lulled into a false sense of security.

Instead of keeping up-to-date, they may slowly become victims of what Mahler (1965) calls 'creeping obsolescence' — where the nature of the job slowly changes and the incumbent slowly ossifies. A different problem faced technically-qualified professionals, such as those in the aerospace industry, when there were drastic cutbacks in government spending. These professionals were working on unique products in a relatively secure environment that was insulated to a large degree from the competition of the market-place. Great difficulty was encountered in making the switch to consumer-orientated products, which required different design, manufacturing, marketing and pricing criteria (Kaufman 1974). Even when managers are employed in dynamic organisations they can still be assigned to work roles that can be either very varied or very stable. Thus the change that they experience in shifting work roles can have an influence on their obsolescence over and above that of the types of organisations in which they are employed.

OUR RESEARCH FINDINGS

Our study examined organisational influences under seven headings as listed here (see questionnaire in Appendix 1). (See Figure 6.1.)

1. Industrial sectors;

2. Company size;

3. Company policy on updating;

4. Company policy on career planning;

5. Rewards for high management performance;

6. Encouragement of innovation;

7. Organisational response to change.

86

```
┌──────────────────────┐
│ Industrial Sector    │
│ Company Size         │
└──────────────────────┘
        ┌────────────────────────────────────┐
        │ Company Policy on Updating         │
        │ Company Policy on Career Planning  │
        └────────────────────────────────────┘
┌──────────────────────────────┐
│ Rewards for Performance      │
│ Encouragement of Innovation  │
└──────────────────────────────┘
        ┌────────────────────────────────────┐
        │ Organisational Response to Change  │
        └────────────────────────────────────┘
```

FIGURE 6.1 *Significant Organisational Influences on Obsolescence*

For detailed statistical information on the relationship between these variables and different aspects of obsolescence, see Appendix 2.

Industrial sectors:

Three sectors of industry were included in out study: Engineering; Food, Drink and Tobacco; and Printing and Paper companies. Engineering companies included those involved in all branches of engineering such as electronics, general engineering, motor car manufacturing and motor garages. Food, Drink and Tobacco companies included those involved in all aspects of food production and processing, drink companies such as those making soft drinks, beers, lagers, spirits and bottling companies, and tobacco companies such as those involved in the manufacturing of various forms of tobacco products like cigarettes, cigars and pipe tobacco. Printing and Paper companies included all those involved in the printing and or publishing of newspapers, magazines and books, book binding and manufacture of paper and paper-based packaging materials such as cartons etc.

The sample included in the study was representative of these three sectors of industry. There were 138 companies in all, divided as follows:

1. Engineering   53
2. Food, Drink and Tobacco   59
3. Printing and Paper   26

The breakdown of managers included from each sector was as follows:

1. Engineering   135
2. Food, Drink and Tobacco   129
3. Printing and Paper   61

This wide diversity of industry was selected because of differences in technology associated with each. These technologies ranged from those which were 'slow changing' such as some food/drink manufacturing, to others which were 'changing rapidly', such as electronics. It was expected that there would be differences between the sectors in terms of obsolescence, for since the demands on the industries varied, these would in turn create different demands on their respective managers.

The results of our study indicated that the greatest degree of obsolescence was experienced by managers in Printing and Paper companies. This finding has serious implications for the industry, which is currently undergoing significant changes in technology.

According to a recent report on the Printing and Paper Industry in Ireland (AnCO 1977), there are two major change areas requiring attention at present. These are in the origination and printing areas. The major shift in origination technology is from hot-metal and stereotyping to cold setting and photo-compository, in addition to lithoplate making and photolithography. The changes in printing technology are mainly from letter press to lithography, flexography and gravure. This report also suggests that greater emphasis will need to be placed on training in areas such as marketing, supervision, cost and estimating, production planning and sales. If this industry hopes to incorporate the new technologies alluded to above and expand in a rapidly changing market, it is essential that its managers are equipped to lead it forward. The results of our study suggest that there is plenty of room for improvement among these managers and supports the recommendation made in the AnCO (1977) report that management development in the Printing and Paper industry be a high priority for the future. The key areas where managers in the Printing and Paper industry felt they could benefit in terms of updating were: Finance (36%); Personnel (18%); Production/Technology (18%) and a broad range of other topics covering human relations, industrial relations, marketing and sales (28%). The most important influences on management development within the industry were: the development of training, technical changes and growth.

Managers from Food, Drink and Tobacco companies rated themselves second highest on obsolescence. This is an industrial sector which has the third largest work force in the country. It is expanding each year, the growth coming both from the introduction of new industry and development of existing industry. Many changes have occurred in recent years, such as the amalgamation of many agricultural co-operatives, the growth in the meat sector and increased processing of home-grown food. There have been similar increases in the drink and tobacco sections of the industry. The main areas where managers in the food, drink and tobacco industry felt they could benefit in terms of updating were: finance (34%), personnel (19%), production/technology (15%), and a variety of other areas such as computerisation, decision-making and human relations (32%). The most important influences on management development within the industry in recent years were: the development of training, growth and changes in the market-place.

Managers from Engineering companies rated themselves the least obsolete of the three sectors. These companies comprised the second largest work force in the country next to

Construction and play a major role in the overall development of UK and Irish industry.

A recent study by Johnston (1976) indicates that there is twice the demand for courses by companies and four times by individuals than are actually available. The demand for management short-term courses is about half that for specialists. Much of the specialist requirements are for post-experience higher degree programmes. This report also indicates that Irish engineering managers spend more than twice their training on science and technology compared with management subjects. They average one week of training every three years. The main areas of need suggested by our study, where managers in engineering companies felt they could benefit were: finance (34%), personnel (18%), production/technology (17%) and a variety of topics such as computerisation, decision-making, planning and human relations (31%).

The major influences on management development within engineering industries in recent years were: the development of training, rapid growth and market changes.

Company size:

Three size ranges of companies were included in our study, 100–249, 250–499 and 500+ employees. In terms of obsolescence rating, it was found that the larger the company, the higher the level of obsolescence. This was an unexpected finding, for the reverse was hypothesised, because it was felt that larger companies would have more facilities and resources available to help managers keep up-to-date.

When the results of the study were discussed with managers, opinion was divided as to the explanations offered. Some managers indicated that those in larger companies who worked in specific functions tended to specialise in a narrow aspect of it e.g. personnel managers may deal only with IR, recruitment/selection or welfare, while in a smaller company they will tend to deal with all aspects of the function. Because of this, they may not be up-to-date on all facets of their particular function. In addition, since there are so many other specialists within their functional area who know more about its different aspects, they realise how out-of-date they are and so rate themselves accordingly. On the other hand, those in smaller companies who carry out all aspects of their function have no one to compare themselves with and so may tend to overrate themselves. The first of these explanations was felt to be the most accurate by a greater number of managers, but to what extent it is actually true is not possible to say without further investigation. The concensus was that managers in smaller companies are forced to keep up-to-date by the very nature of their work, in that more depends on them than in a larger company. This feeling was expressed by many managers from all sizes of companies.

Company policy on updating:
Organisational policy on updating was found to be related to managerial obsolescence, but not very strongly. The results showed that Engineering companies were the most likely to have a policy in relation to updating of their staff.

In fact, the sequence of responses to this question indicates the same pattern as that for obsolescence ratings: that managers who rated themselves the most obsolete were from Printing and Paper companies, which were also the least likely to have a policy regarding updating of staff. On the other hand, managers from Engineering companies rated themselves the least obsolete and, as noted, these companies were most likely to have a policy for updating staff. There was, therefore, a high correlation between obsolescence rating and presence or absence of a policy for updating staff, but it was not statistically significant.

The results of our study indicate, however, that the presence of a company policy on updating did not affect its managers participation in updating activities. In fact, the reverse was the case. Managers from Printing and Paper companies were more likely to be influenced by such a policy (although they were least likely to have one) than managers from Engineering companies (who were most likely to have one). Perhaps the explanation for this lies in the suggestion that when a policy is readily available, managers do not appreciate it and it is taken for granted, while when policies are not readily available managers tend to maximise their use. It seems that in general, *what is not available is sought, while what is available is ignored.*

Company policy on career planning:
Our results show that there is a significant relationship between the presence of an organisational policy on career planning and managerial obsolescence.

Engineering companies provided the greatest incentives to staff for updating, such as payment of fees, time off for study and recognition on completion of studies. Printing and Paper companies provided the least incentive to staff and were least likely to assist in the payment of fees or provide encouragement to staff.

Dubin and Marlow (1965) found that 79% of engineers in their study reported that their companies had educational assistance programmes, but 74% reported that this availability had no effect on motivating them to undertake additional work. Similarly, 49% of middle managers said that company policy on financial aid had little effect on their decision to undertake further education (Dubin, Alderman and Marlow 1967). Further evidence derived from these studies indicated that taking additional course work was not sufficiently rewarded in industry and was not a requirement for promotion or salary increase. Rothman and Perrucci (1971) found that when attendance at professional activities was rewarded by organisations, it was not associated with low levels of obsolescence.

Printing and Paper companies were the most likely to carry out long-term career planning for their management staff. The least likely were Engineering companies. Over half (54%) of the sample indicated that their companies did not carry out long-term career planning for their managers. This perhaps explains why so many managers are not influenced by company policy on updating. They see little *point in it unless there is a pay-off for doing so.* This will be discussed in the next section. There is inconsistency in regard to career planning, for Engineering companies were the most likely to have a policy for updating, while they were least likely to have a policy for career planning. It seems that it is thought to be appropriate to encourage managers to update, but not to plan for their future careers. Printing and Paper companies, on the other hand, were most likely to plan for managers' careers, but least likely to have a policy for updating.

Many writers indicate that managers must be given stimulating jobs if they are to be encouraged to update (Kaufman 1974, Van Atta *et al.* 1970 and Hall 1971). One of the greatest problems identified by Kaufman (1974) is what he calls the under-utilisation or mis-utilisation of managers' skills and abilities. It seems essential that if managers are to be given satisfying work, then some career planning is necessary. However, most companies do not seem to invest much effort in this regard and hence contribute to managerial obsolescence inadvertently. This seems to be corroborated by the finding that managers in Engineering companies found their jobs the least challenging, while these same companies were least likely to carry out career planning.

Rewards for high management performance:
Rewards for high management performance were found to be significantly related to managerial obsolescence.

Half of the respondents indicated that their companies rewarded high management performance. This was found to be the case mainly in Printing and Paper companies, which were most likely to carry out career planning for their managers. Managers from Food, Drink and Tobacco companies were least likely to be rewarded for high performance.

Thompson and Dalton (1976) suggest that rewards are designed as an incentive to engineers in R & D organisations to move into management and away from technical work. Horgan and Floyd (1971) indicate that the type of rewards which are important to managers include the opportunity to use newly acquired knowledge and skills, promotion and an increase in personal security. Rand (1977) suggests that before any reward system is developed, organisations should examine what types of rewards are most appropriate and what they should be given for, in addition to ensuring that they are equitably distributed amongst staff. The main emphasis should be on treating managers as individuals and rewarding them accordingly for work well done (Lawler 1974).

Encouragement of innovation:
The results of our study show that encouragement of innovation among managers was also significantly related to obsolescence. Managers from Engineering companies indicated that their companies were the most likely to encourage innovation. Engineering companies were also the second most likely to reward high management performance, but were least likely to have challenging jobs for their managers. The least likely to encourage innovation were Food, Drink and Tobacco companies, yet they had the most challenging jobs for their managers. This suggests that job challenge and encouragement are not very highly correlated.

A number of writers indicated that innovation is important to keep managers stimulated (Dalton *et al.* 1977). There are a number of ways of encouraging this, such as giving managers new problems to solve, job rotation, secondments and working on task-forces to deal with short-term emergencies. Van Atta *et al.* (1970) suggest that companies plan effective management programmes in order to maintain the technical vitality of their staff. This ensures that company problems are creatively dealt with. Such companies are characterised by 'high productivity, excitement and sense of purpose' according to Miller (1972).

Organisational response to change:
Organisational response to change was found to be significantly related to obsolescence. Printing and Paper companies were found to be the best at responding to change. Perhaps this is a reflection of the rapid technological changes taking place in this industry in recent years. A surprising feature of this result is that the greatest degree of obsolescence among managers was found to be in this industry, although it is good at responding to change. Perhaps this is explained by the fact that when a company undergoes rapid change, then its managers become more conscious of their short-comings and the need for updating; on the other hand, when a company is in a period of stabilisation the managers may not fully realise the importance of updating to the same degree.

Food, Drink and Tobacco companies were found to be the least capable of responding to change. These companies were also least likely to reward high management performance or encourage innovation, but yet had the most challenging jobs (according to their managers).

Rothman and Perrucci (1970) indicate that managers employed in industries characterised by rapid technological change acquire a greater amount of new knowledge than do those who work in less dynamic environments. The incidence of obsolescence was also found to be less for managers in companies that experience a high growth rate. The results of our study would appear to be at variance with these reports, but perhaps the reason for this lies in the fact that some managers can be assigned to routine work roles with little variation even in dynamic organisations (Kaufman 1974). Thus the actual work roles that managers occupy can have an influence on their obsolescence over and above that of the organisations in which they work.

Engineering companies were second best at responding to change, but best at encouraging innovation, which illustrates the points made above.

CHAPTER 7

Coping with Obsolescence: The Training Implications

Coping with obsolescence will be dealt with under three headings (see Figure 7.1):

1. The individual manager;

2. The organisation;

3. Management development.

THE INDIVIDUAL MANAGER

It has been pointed out earlier in Chapter 2 that there is much contradictory research evidence regarding the influence of age on obsolescence. Lehman (1963), Pelz and Andrews (1966) and Dalton and Thompson (1971) have all reported that managers' and engineers'/scientists' performance tends to decrease with age after the mid-thirties. Up to then performance was improving, then peaked and gradually went into decline. This varied, depending on the type of work engaged in and attitude towards such factors as learning,

FIGURE 7.1 *A Model for Coping With or Combating Obsolescence*

change and updating activities. Van Atta *et al.* (1970), however, report that there is much evidence to suggest that managers' performance does not alter appreciably provided they work in a stimulating environment, which is conducive to personal growth and development, provides a variety of work experiences and encourages continuous updating of skills and knowledge. Furthermore, an important variable in favour of age is the wealth of experience a manager gains throughout his career. This, coupled with the numerous business contacts and acquaintances, are also tremendously helpful in keeping a manager's performance level high.

The results of our particular study indicate that managers' age, educational attainment and professional/technical qualifications are not major influences on managerial obsolescence. Neither is their engagement in any single updating activity. The variables that are important, however, are their perception of their learning ability and how important they perceive it is to keep up-to-date. Both of these appear to influence significantly their level of obsolescence.

These findings suggest that if managers are to cope with or prevent the onset of obsolescence, they must be helped to recognise themselves as learners and develop a positive perception of their learning ability. This includes helping them to enjoy new learning experiences, which can be done by minimising the fear of a threatening environment or by sending them on courses or development programmes which they choose themselves. The most effective updating activities that managers engaged in were educational programmes in their own time. These were self-chosen and in many cases were paid for out of their own pockets. It does not appear to be very effective to send managers on programmes that they do not wish to go on, particularly if they feel that they do not have the mental ability to cope with them.

Obsolescent managers indicated that they had difficulty keeping up with professional literature in their field. These difficulties were mainly due to lack of time, but some managers also said that they could not understand the jargon being used in modern books and journals and felt that the ideas being presented were difficult to comprehend.

The obsolescent managers were least likely to belong to a professional association and hence could not benefit from the various services provided. This is turn meant that they did not have the same opportunities of meeting with their peers to discuss common problems, as those who were active in such associations. Perhaps then, it might be important to encourage managers to become members of relevant associations and facilitate their attendance at professional meetings.

The key elements in helping managers to cope with or prevent the onset of obsolescence are to engage in continuous learning activities whether formal or informal, to move from passive (reading, attending lectures etc.) to active learning (on-the-job problem-solving, assignment, project work etc.) and change from learning of facts to *learning to learn*. These involve taking responsibility for one's own destiny and moving from a lagging-behind practice to one of leadership. These suggestions are also made by Ansoff (1973) when commenting on the future of management education. He suggests that the future lies in:

1. convergence of the public and private sector;

2. product differentiation;

3. new institutional arrangements;

4. change from episodic to career-long learning;

5. change from passive to active, participative learning;

6. change from a keeping-up practice to leadership;

7. change from uniconstituency to multiconstituency management.

THE ORGANISATION

A number of suggestions have been made by Thompson and Dalton (1976) to help organisations cope with the impending obsolescence of their managerial staff. These focus on barriers to mobility which prevent managers moving from one 'stage' to the next. These have become exacerbated in the 1970s due to slower growth, which means fewer promotions, fewer transfers, fewer people leaving and fewer people being hired. They caution organisations on the possibility of stagnation through immobility. To prevent this requires a conscious strategy to facilitate movement of people between jobs. Although this is recognised as important to maintain an organisation's dynamism, it sometimes cannot do much about it due to a number of barriers that have grown up. Some of those can be removed by:

1. *limiting tenure in managerial positions* so that managers can be shifted about more easily and thus prevent the attitude developing that if an individual gets a management position, he can expect to stay there indefinitely;

2. making more effective use of *lateral transfers* can help to increase motivation and promote innovation through challenging job assignments;

3. *manpower reviews* can be helpful, by identifying individuals who are becoming obsolete and shifting them to new jobs;

4. *career monitoring* ensures that managers are not allowed to stay in one place too long, or alternatively, not allowed to overspecialise in too narrow a field of work, making them unsuitable for the future job changes.

A somewhat different approach is proposed by Horgan and Floyd (1971), who make the following suggestions to help companies develop an anti-obsolescence policy; the questions that need to be asked are:

1. What are the short-range and intermediate-range goals of the organisation in terms of manpower planning for the technical disciplines?;

2. Have the goals of the organisation been defined in terms of overall product and personnel objectives, as well as the interrelation between the various technical activities?;

3. What are the changing technological fields that are likely to assume a significant role within the organisation during the next five to ten years?;

4. Where in the organisation are the areas of critical need?;

5. How will any proposed programmes help individuals to become more effective within the company? What

effect will the proposed training have on the way an individual will perform his job?;

6. Will the organisation be able to absorb the retrained individual effectively and make use of his newly acquired knowledge?

Further suggestions by Reeser (1977) are that organisations should take unilateral action on the following if they are to deal effectively with obsolescence. These include:

1. Outright termination of those who have become obsolescent and are no longer productive in organisational terms;

2. Demotion should also be considered although it is not very common and is often seen to have a denigrating effect on the individual. However, it may well be the lesser of two evils;

3. Early retirement can be considered for those in their mid-fifties and beyond and can be a mutually beneficial way of solving the problem;

4. 'Kicking the guy upstairs' can be used if the manager is too young to retire; this centres around giving the individual a certain amount of dignity and prestige while at the same time keeping him out of the way of significant decisions and from obstructing capable people; and

5. Internal advertising of job openings which can sometimes shake obsolescent employees into doing something to get out of the rut they find themselves in.

(Reeser 1977)

A novel and imaginative solution to obsolescence has been proposed by Connor and Fielden (1973), in which the organisation and the individual pool their efforts to solve the problem. The scheme involves the organisation making it possible for the individual to prepare for a second career in case he or she becomes surplus by granting a number of educational credits for each year of service. These are redeemable in cash after a stipulated period of time with the company, thus enabling the individual to return for further education and/or study for a new career. Although this may be costly for the organisation, it may work out cheaper than keeping an unproductive manager on the payroll. It can of course cause great upset for the individual, but perhaps not as much as that caused by termination, demotion or having to prepare for alternative employment, unaided. Another suggestion to help organisations and obsolescent managers was made by Schultz (1974), which consists of the establishment of *mid-career clinics* which would be used to examine each manager's individual case and make appropriate recommendations. This examination would include a study of past performance reviews, interviews with the person and his subordinates, peers and superiors. These would be used to isolate each manager's defects and strengths, and point to actions needed to correct defects and capitalise on strengths. Farris (1973) also suggests a number of managerial strategies to motivate performance in a particular type of organisation. These are shown in Figure 7.2.

Results of our study further indicate that there are many implications for organisations if they are to help cope with or prevent the onset of managerial obsolescence. These implications are of two kinds: those associated with managerial jobs and those associated with the organisation itself.

In terms of managerial obsolescence, we found that the incidence or degree of obsolescence varied by function, with those in Production and R & D positions rating themselves the most obsolete, while the opposite was true of those in Finance and Personnel. This suggests that special attention should be paid to Production and R & D managers to help their professional development and growth.

Managers at different levels also appeared to experience obsolescence of varying degrees, with those at junior/middle management the worst. This finding emphasises the need for planned professional development of the managers early on in their careers in order to maintain the updating momentum.

Job challenge appears to be a major variable in relation to

Factor	Move from Disaster, Atrophy, Stagnation	To Opportunity Maturity, Renewal
Career Opportunities		
1. Job Security	Unclear	Clear
2. Professional Growth opportunities	Unclear no programme	Professional Growth programme
Inofrmal Organisation		
3. Technical Collaboration	Low	High
4. Technical Teams	Old	Re-grouping of Teams
5. 'Key Persons'	Unrecognised	Recognised
6. Internal Contacts	Limited	Extensive
7. External Contacts	Limited	Extensive
Work Goals		
8. Work Assignments	Single Task	Multiple tasks
9. Time pressure	Low	High
10. Consequences of good performance	Unclear	Greater challenge

FIGURE 7.2 *Some Managerial Strategies to Motivate Performance in a Stable Organisation*

managerial obsolescence. Associated with this are functional and company decision-making, and the extent to which jobs utilise managers' skills and abilities. Managers with challenging jobs were significantly less obsolete than those without, which reinforces the earlier arguments that managers be given challenging, stimulating and rewarding work. This will likely go a long way towards helping them to remain up-to-date.

This can be done partly by encouraging managers to be innovative and rewarding high management performance, both of which were also significantly related to managerial obsolescence. Furthermore, it seems to be important for organisations to have a policy with regard to long-term career planning for management staff. This can ensure that managers continue to remain up-to-date by assigning appropriate duties which will require continuous learning and development.

Organisations that are poor at responding to change have been found to have the most obsolescent managers, which suggests that managers in more dynamic organisations are less likely to experience high levels of obsolescence. This result indicates that organisations should examine themselves periodically, if not continuously, to see how well they are capable of responding to change whether from outside or within. Those that are inflexible or resistant to change should take cognisance of the fact and be aware of the likely effects of this on their managers' ability to keep up-to-date.

Finally, it is also important for managers in organisations to take an interest in their subordinates' growth and development. This can be done by various means, such as informal or formal discussions, encouraging them to engage in updating activities and providing the facilities and resources for them to do so. This appears to be required at all levels of management in order to reduce the overall effects of managerial obsolescence in the organisation.

Large companies should be particularly aware of their influences on managerial obsolescence, especially in relation to overspecialisation or narrowing of functions. Care needs to be taken in these organisations that managers do not get 'lost' in the system, by being assigned to routine or narrow jobs, especially in administration. Some ways of coping with this include job rotation, secondments to other plants or organisations, job enrichment, project assignments or special task-force commitments.

Some variables which were found not to be significantly related to managerial obsolescence were, whether companies had a policy in relation to continuing/further education and training of their staff, or whether they provide financial assistance for them. The extent to which managers' personal decisions to update were influenced by company policy was not significantly related to managerial obsolescence, neither was the type of updating activity engaged in.

The most important influences on management development in recent years were changes in job demands, external factors and the establishment of a training function within the company under the influence of government training authorities (TSD, AnCO, etc.). These findings are illustrated by the following comments of managers:

1. 'A major re-equipment programme, coupled with the recession here made our company place greater emphasis on training for management' (Senior Financial Manager);

2. 'The recession caused a major re-appraisal of the company's future growth and development' (Board level Financial Manager);

3. 'Development of new product and export markets' (Senior Production Manager);

4. 'Pressure from parent firm and formalisation of training' (Middle level Personnel Manager);

5. 'Encouragement of top management to have people kept up-to-date' (Middle level Financial Manager);

6. 'Growth of activities and development of company infra-structure, foreign business and technological change' (Senior Financial Manager);

7. 'AnCO Levy Grant System, I do not believe our company would exist today if we did not attend management programmes' (Board level Production Manager);

8. 'Growth of company activities over past 10—12 years high-lighted lack of management skills in many areas' (Senior Personnel Manager);

9. 'The integration of training with long-term managerial development, based on appraisal and identification of training needs' (Senior Financial Manager);

10; 'The necessity of training to keep up-to-date so as to hold existing markets and to produce a product which can compete' (Senior Personnel Manager).

In reference to the general question of Irish and UK managers keeping up-to-date, the most frequent comments made were that they need more training. This is exemplified in such comments as:

1. 'Our managers still tend to be very similar and would benefit from overseas experience through secondment or courses' (Senior Production Manager);

2. 'It would appear to me that managers do not allocate sufficient time to keeping up-to-date, either because they are unaware of not being up-to-date or not sufficient courses are available' (Senior Production Manager);

3. 'As business is continually becoming more complicated, continuous training is essential' (Board level Financial Manager);

4. 'Very important that they do, whether encouraged or not — few medium firms see benefit in courses and family firms, not at all, or possibly only for family members' (Middle Manager, Personnel);

5. 'They seem to get too involved in day-to-day functions and do not devote enough time to keeping up-to-date and learning new skills and techniques (Senior Financial Manager).

These sets of responses indicate the need for organisations and individuals to recognise the importance of updating and the necessity for continued development in order to deal effectively with the constant changes affecting industry today.

MANAGEMENT DEVELOPMENT

Continuing education and other formal training programmes have been traditional ways of helping managers keep up-to-date according to many studies of obsolescence. Other evidence by Saunders *et al.* (1974) indicates that there has also been a tremendous growth in in-company type courses which are tailor-made for companies because universities and colleges were not providing the relevant type of training for active managers. A major difficulty with all these formal types of programmes is that they are often designed by management specialists without adequate prior consultation with participants. Another difficulty is that many managers are sent on these programmes for a variety of reasons unrelated to training, such as 'getting the guy out-of-the-way for a while', 'giving the manager a break from the job after completing a tough assignment', using a course as a perk, status boost or morale boost instead of genuine development or lastly, sending a manager on a course which is either irrelevant or of no interest to him. These are common abuses of courses, however good they may be, so that objectively they do not often benefit the participant at all, or at least very little. There is much evidence to suggest that the most effective use of courses seems to be made by managers who elect to go on them themselves rather than being told to do so.

A wide variety of updating activities were dealt with in our study, yet attendance or participation in any of these was not significantly related to managerial obsolescence. The most commonly engaged in activities were reading work-related books and journals, on-the-job problem-solving and attending seminars and conferences. The most useful activities according to managers were educational pro-grammes in their own time, on-the-job problem-solving and attending external training programmes. These results emphasise the importance of managers taking control of their own development and selecting their own approach to help them update. *Our* results also indicate that the *informal and continuous method of updating in the form of on-the-job problem-solving was more effective than more formal periodic methods such as attending courses, seminars, conferences and such like.* External courses were found to be more helpful than in-company courses. These findings are important for managers and their organisations to recognise, if they hope to ward off or cope with the onset of managerial obsolescence. It is not going to be dealt with by sending

107

managers on the occasional training course or seminar. It requires more organised and long-term commitment to providing challenging work which will facilitate development through everyday problem-solving. The use of courses and other such approaches may be helpful as additional aids, but they may only be useful in a complementary sense.

In order to help managers to keep up-to-date and/or cope with the problems of obsolescence it is necessary to identify what knowledge areas they feel they could benefit from (see Figure 7.3). The most important areas mentioned by managers in our study were personnel/industrial relations and finance (both 30%). Personnel was divided into a number of sub-topics such as 'selection interviewing', 'staff training and development', 'selection testing', and 'labour legislation'. In the case of industrial relations, the main topics were 'negotiation skills' and help in the development

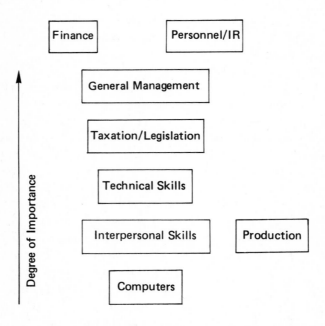

FIGURE 7.3 *Subjects Requiring Most Updating*

108

of 'conflict resolution skills'. A number of topics were included under finance, such as various 'accounting procedures', 'corporate finance', and 'company law'. General management and taxation/legislation were mentioned by 16% and 14% of managers respectively. This emphasis on taxation/legislation was brought about by EEC regulations. Mention was made of such topics as EEC directives, regulations governing the quality of goods, processing procedures (especially in Food, Drink and Tobacco companies) and the use of various materials. Taxation was seen to be important, especially in relation to the importing/exporting of goods.

The general management skills identified included a greater knowledge of the principles of management, man-management and administrative skills. Other topics were organisation development, planning, manpower utilisation, decision-making and delegation of responsibilities. Technical skills were mentioned by 12% of the managers, and included such topics as engineering, maintenance, new developments in industrial technology (e.g. plastics and chemicals) and quality control.

Interpersonal skills were identified by 7% of the managers from various functions. These skills centred mainly on communications, motivation and the contribution of the behavioural sciences to management.

Production knowledge was mentioned by a further 7%. This included production scheduling and control, work study, materials handling and stock control. These were mainly the concern of production managers.

Computers were identified by 6% of respondents, mainly those in finance. They felt that perhaps they could make better use of computers in their work, but were not fully conversant with their applications.

Ten per cent mentioned a wide range of other topics such as sales, marketing, languages and a variety of educational programmes.

These results have wide implications for any intervention programme developed to help managers cope with updating problems. There appears to be a big need for further training, especially in finance and personnel. Whether this reflects insufficient training available on these topics, or whether what is available is inappropriate is not possible to say, but it has implications for those providing training and development to ensure they supply an adequate range of courses in these subjects. This also raises the question of how organisations and managers can best cope with changes arising in these subjects. Professional associations have a role to play in helping their members keep up-to-date through newsletters, seminars and professional meetings which are used for this purpose rather than merely social occasions.

The topics mentioned by up-to-date managers were mainly personnel, taxation and technology, while for those high on obsolescence the main topics were finance, technology and interpersonal skills. According to Dubin, Alderman and Marlow (1967) the most important topics rated by senior managers were finance and communications, while for middle managers the main areas were classified broadly as management development and working efficiently with others. Other writers do not appear to have addressed this question at all. Instead, they have investigated the type of learning approach most suited to managers, rather than identifying the most beneficial learning content for managers.

The findings of our study also suggest that managers need to keep a constant watch on areas they might be neglecting. This can be done by carrying out an assessment of training needs at regular intervals. A number of approaches have been put forward to help managers do this. These are well-documented and elucidated in Pedler, Burgoyne and Boydell's book *A Manager's Guide to Self-Development* (1978) which can be used by individual managers either on their own or in small groups, and at any time. The techniques can also be repeated at regular intervals and still provide useful input on development needs. Once identified, these needs can then be tackled in an appropriate fashion.

One final point of note is that UK and Irish managers and organisations need to be more creative in their approach to coping with managerial obsolescence. US companies use many forms of updating such as work-planning seminars, after-hours education, special courses (tailor-made to individual needs), relocating staff, demotion, promotion, lateral transfer, shoring up (providing an assistant), psychological and medical assistance (Haas 1968). These are far more diverse than is likely to be found in the UK or Ireland, but perhaps this is explained by the difference in company size, range and culture.

The whole aim of these measures is to develop resourceful managers who can and will take control of their own development (Morris and Burgoyne 1973).

CHAPTER 8

Managerial Obsolescence: The Future

In a large-scale study of executive obsolescence carried out by the American Management Association (1968), 74% of companies surveyed said they had a problem with it. Many indicated that 20—25% of their executives showed effects of obsolescence. 60% of the companies had active management development programmes in operation. Methods used by 50% of the companies included: continuing education programmes, executive promotions, rotation and demotion, medical check-ups and correction programmes. Other methods used in the event of obsolescence were reduction in authority, redevelopment, transfer or relocation, termination and the provision of assistants to take over responsibilities. There was a great deal of emphasis placed on career development programmes to help managers cope with obsolescence difficulties, but these have come into question as a result of the work of Dalton *et al.* (1977). They have indicated that millions are spent each year on continuing education programmes in companies and universities, but the results of these do not always justify the costs. In addition, a variety of professional groups have pressed for legislation in the US that would require continuing education as the price of continuing professional practice. They cite examples of lawyers in Minnesota who are required to take the equivalent of 15 course hours a year to avoid being placed on a restricted status, and the Engineering Foundation of Ohio who have recently suggested a law requiring almost the same qualification of engineers. Accountants in several US states currently face the possibility of having to return to the classroom in order to retain their professional status. This is not confined to the US alone, for the French Atomic Energy Commission recently initiated the practice of declaring that scientific diplomas lapse after five years, unless revalidated by attendance at refresher courses and success in passing further examinations (*Ford Foundation Report* 1967). The US National Advisory Commission on Health Manpower (1967) recommended that 'professional societies and state governments should explore the possibility of periodic relicensing of physicians and other health professionals. This should be granted either upon certification of acceptable performance in continuing education programmes, or upon the basis of challenge examinations in a practitioner's speciality'. The Oregon Medical Association (USA) passed a regulation arising from this, requiring physicians to continue their education in order to remain in good standing with the Association.

ORGANISATIONAL RESPONSE TO OBSOLESCENCE

The typical organisational response to deal with obsolescence has been to provide or support a host of continuing education programmes for its management staff. The varying kinds of activities being undertaken by some US organisations to maintain technical vitality are illustrated in Table 8.1.

There is little disagreement that some type of continuing education is necessary for updating, upgrading, or diversifying one's knowledge and skills in order to maintain currency of knowledge and skills for present jobs. Although most

Table 8.1 *List of Activities Currently Sponsored by US Organisations*

Activity	Percentage of Organisations sponsoring it
Tuition refund Plan	90
Attendance at Professional and Technical Society Meetings	67
External Technical Lectures	62
In-plant Courses	57
Educational Leave Plan	37
Research and Teaching by Employees	30
Post-doctoral Training	0.6

Source: Committee on Utilisation of Scientific and Engineering Manpower 1964.

organisations provide their own programmes or encourage their managers to participate in external ones, the effectiveness of these have been brought into question in recent times. Wheeler's (1968) study of continuing education courses for engineers and scientists revealed shortcomings in the management of these courses in terms of their organisation, participation and assessment which limit their anti-obsolescence effectiveness. Landis (1969) summarises the results of a similar survey as follows:

1. Most engineers are not interested in continuing education; they are interested in how to do their current job better. They will respond to training rather than to education and they will demand an almost immediate payoff in terms of recognition or salary;

114

2. The contribution of most engineers to their company may have little to do with their expertise in engineering. Most men, especially as they grow older, do not look for intellectual challenge but rather how to do the job faster and easier;

3. Even though corporate management may have expressed a real interest in continuing education, it is the immediate supervisor who counts. Unless he is willing to encourage and accommodate his subordinates, in spite of the possible interference in work schedules, few men will undertake continuing studies;

4. Continuing education planning has frequently been a haphazard effort by enterprising colleges, companies and professional societies. Further development will require a closer relationship between industry and the colleges;

5. There is a need to establish a better intellectual climate in many companies if it is hoped to benefit from continuing education programmes.

Kaufman (1975) examined in-company and university-sponsored courses for engineers, with respect to the factors influencing participation, as well as the effects of course-taking on subsequent technical competence. His findings report that:

1. The primary objective for most engineers to participate in continuing education is to keep from becoming obsolete and not to obtain an advanced degree as is often assumed. Engineers' course-taking objectives are oriented towards future career development rather than immediate job needs;

2. Participation in graduate courses tends to be by engineers who are the most competent and more theoretically-oriented to begin with, whereas in-company courses are more frequently taken by those with opposite characteristics;

3. The nature of the work can affect course-taking behaviour. Work which requires the utilisation of engineering knowledge and skills tends to stimulate graduate enrolment, regardless of the engineers' competence. However, those who have only a limited utilisation of their knowledge and skills tend to take more in-company courses, perhaps in an attempt to make up for a lack of professional stimulation and challenge in their work, or to reduce their anxiety about becoming obsolete;

4. A frustrating organisational climate can affect course-taking behaviour. Engineers whose needs are frustrated by organisational constraints may turn to courses in an attempt to satisfy such needs;

5. Graduate courses are clearly more effective in keeping engineers from becoming obsolete than are in-company courses.

He concludes by stating that organisations must devote more careful efforts towards planning, implementing and assessing their continuing education programmes if they are to be helpful in satisfying the development needs of both the individual managers and their organisations.

An investigation by Dalton and Thompson (1971) also showed that courses alone are not an effective remedy to obsolescence. For example:

1. When we correlated performance rankings of engineers with courses taken in the previous three years, there was no relationship. In nearly all age groups, the courses did not seem to help.

2. In one company, we found that the engineers over 40 who needed and were taking company-sponsored courses were the very ones whose performance ratings declined from year to year.

3. Another company in our study spent more time and money than any other to provide continuing education for its engineers and scientists. But this company's obsolescence problem was just as serious as that of the others.

According to Saunders *et al.* (1974), the growth of in-company continuing education courses has been spurred on by a variety of factors such as the fact that many colleges and universities do not offer the courses required by industry or if they do, the courses are too theoretical and not applicable to industrial situations, or they are held at times which are unsuitable for employed personnel. If a company provides its own programmes, it can tailor them to specific company needs and hire top experts to run them at convenient times. However, before designing any continuing education programmes it is first necessary to identify and determine the

116

education/training needs of management. Knowles (1970) suggests that this can be done through interviews, questionnaires, tests, group problem analysis, performance appraisals and management by objectives. Van Atta *et al.* (1970) describe one approach used by the Battelle Memorial Institute Columbus (USA), a major R & D research organisation, for developing a career planning programme. Each staff member was asked to describe his ultimate career objectives, then his supervisor performed a similar function for that individual and then counselled with him, and together they compared career objectives and plans. If there was agreement between the two, then they proceeded to prepare a career development plan for the staff member. If there was a discrepancy, it was checked out carefully as it was felt to be crucial to clear up any misunderstandings at this point. This was especially so for those in mid-career, where the future may not look as promising as it did at an earlier time. The reason why an organisation like Battelle would go to so much trouble to plan an effective career development programme for its management staff was because an organisation's technical vitality is measured by the knowledge of its staff and their ability to put that knowledge creatively to work to meet the objectives of the organisation. Such an organisation according to Miller (1972) 'is characterised by high productivity, excitement, sense of purpose, feeling of accomplishment, a sense of personal opportunity, openness to change and new ideas, nearly unachievable goals, fair and thoughtful measurement, appropriate recognition and reward, and strong contacts with ideas and people outside the organisation'.

MOTIVATION TO UPDATE

For many managers the motivation to engage in continuing education or career development programmes lies in what they see as the payoff at the end. If they cannot perceive any advantages, they will not be very stimulated to exert the effort necessary to engage in further learning. This is in line with what Landis (1969) found, as quoted earlier. The importance of recognition and reward among scientific and technical personnel has also been noted by Glaser (1963) and Marcson (1960). Hughes and Wass (1970) describe a company-installed management policy in which goal-oriented management behaviour is rewarded by task satisfaction, financial rewards and goal accomplishment. The system provides a means for continuous updating of employees in that individual goal setting is integrated with the organisation's goal setting. This is accomplished through the use of semi-annual goal-oriented performance reviews in which each employee participates.

Many companies have educational assistance funds which reimburse employees who undertake continuing education courses, but few make it mandatory to do so. In their Pennsylvania State University study, Dubin and Marlow (1965) note that 79% of engineers reported that their companies had educational assistance programmes, showing the widespread availability of company payment for educational courses, but 74% of engineers reported that this availability had no effect in motivating them to undertake additional work. Similarly, 49% of middle managers (Dubin, Alderman and Marlow 1967) said that company policy on financial aid had little effect on their decision to undertake further education. Further evidence derived from these studies indicated that taking additional course work was not sufficiently rewarded in industry and was not a requirement for promotion or salary increase. The availabilty of financial assistance for self-improvement is obviously not a sufficient incentive for employees to update.

Rothman and Perrucci (1971) tested the hypothesis that, 'where an organisational atmosphere in which professional activities related to coping with obsolescence were regularly rewarded, this would be associated with lower rates of obsolescence than one in which such activity was not rewarded'. Their findings indicated that this hypothesis was not tenable.

They state, however, that this finding may be produced by the effect of certain intervening variables, which mitigate the effects of a positive policy. One of these is the existence of a discrepancy between official policies and the translation of such policies into practice by first-line managers. Another possibility is that engineers are sometimes unaware of these policies or do not perceive the articulation of them. Whatever the cause, it is apparent that a policy of rewards is not, in itself, sufficient to significantly weaken vulnerability to obsolescence.

REWARDS FOR PERFORMANCE

Thompson and Dalton (1976) commenting on reward systems suggest that in some R & D organisations the reward system is designed to provide an incentive to the brightest people to move out of technical work and into management. This defines those who have been promoted into management as winners and those still performing the prime task of the organisation as losers. In such situations, it is difficult for the technical professional to take pride in his work, when all the power and status go to the managers. If an organisation is going to keep talented people doing technical work, it must provide meaningful rewards to high-performing personnel. This can be done in a number of ways such as providing pay for performance, not position, recognising individuals' contribution to important decision-making and encouraging them to make presentations to the chief executive and outside groups, thus increasing their 'visibility' both within and without the organisation. Other rewards mentioned by Horgan and Floyd (1971) include the opportunity to use newly acquired knowledge and skills, promotions, and an increase in the sense of personal security.

Before any reward system is developed by an organisation, Rand (1977) makes the following points:

1. The magnitude of rewards must satisfy the basic human needs of survival and security;

119

2. Organisations must choose relevant rewards over which they have the potential capability to provide and manipulate;

3. The distribution of rewards among employees must be perceived as being done in a fair and equitable manner;

4. Organisational members must perceive a 'link' or a contingency between their job performance and the rewards they receive; and

5. A reward or variety of rewards used by an organisation must be valued by the individual members of that organisation.

This approach to rewards requires organisations to treat employees as individuals which, although difficult, and perhaps requiring a break with much prior tradition, is receiving ever-increasing support from the behavioural sciences. As Lawler (1974) puts it:

> Work can be made a more rewarding place to be, and organisations can be made more effective, if approaches to organisation design treat employees as individuals . . . What we need, then, are ways of running organisations that recognise the importance of treating people differently and placing them in environments and work situations that fit their unique needs, skills and abilities.

What then are the updating activities which managers have found to be the most effective? This is answered somewhat by Margulies and Raia (1967) who asked a similar question of scientists and engineers. The responses were: on-the-job problem-solving (42%); on-the-job colleague interaction (20%); publishing and independent reading (16%); formal courses (14%); and outside professional activities (4%). A related study be Randle (1959) reported broadly similar findings, in that 85% of professional development was attributed to on-the-job experience.

'Communications' techniques' and 'financial management' were the two topics rated as most wanted by senior management respondents in Dubin, Alderman and Marlow's (1967) study. The majority of middle managers reported that they would be willing to enrol in credit (67%) and non-credit

(77%) courses if they were available locally. The particular topics that they felt they *should have* were 'management development' (66%) and 'working efficiently with individuals' (65%). The results of this study have been dealt with in the previous chapter.

Kaufman (1974) in his book on obsolescence concluded that . . . 'the single most important stimulation for professional development and growth is on-the-job problem-solving that often requires a diversity of challenging work assignments'. He added: 'Since the main contributor to obsolescence is the work itself and how it is organised, management can reorganise the professional's job in order to stimulate the utilisation of knowledge and skills and instil a desire to stay abreast of new developments. A re-organisation of work can be attained by using such techniques as job design and enrichment'.

Current practice of scientists and engineers of some major employers outlined in a recent issue of IEEE Transactions on Education (1976) would seem to indicate that on-the-job problem-solving has in fact been chosen as the single most effective way of keeping professionals up-to-date.

INDUSTRIAL SABBATICALS

'Industrial sabbaticals' are encouraged by Evan (1963) and Dalton and Thompson (1971), for although they might appear expensive, they may be the most effective way of combating obsolescence (see Table 8.2). This is based on their findings that engineers who complete graduate courses are rated higher than those without. In fact, the performance ratings of engineers with masters degrees hold up ten years longer than for those with bachelor degrees. Other methods suggested were to look carefully at job assignments, for it could be very beneficial for engineers to be assigned to new fields at about 35—40 years of age. Many indicate that they become bored after 15—20 years at the same work, while a new field of interest might whet their appetite and encourage

Table 8.2 *Types of Industrial Sabbaticals and their Potential Benefits*

Types of Sabbaticals	Benefits
To Universities or Institutes of Higher Learning	Opportunity to view career and work from a distance. Opportunity to study and update knowledge in particular fields. Opportunity to apply theory to practice based on work experiences.
To Government or Quasi-Government Agencies	Opportunity to apply skills to national problems. Opportunity to work with the power base of the country.
To Management Consultancies	Opportunity to work in other companies and learn how they operate.
To Companies in the Same/or Related Industry	Opportunity to check out current knowledge/skills and develop new ones.
To Client Companies	Opportunity to see how own company's products are utilised. Opportunity to assist client company in the development of new application of own company's products.
To Other Functions	Opportunity to broaden management experience.
From HQ to Company Branches or *vice versa*	Opportunity to examine and learn how others in the organisation ('the other half') do things.

them to seek further training and development to improve their competency. These suggestions are also made by Kaufman (1974) and Miller (1972).

Dunnette and Campbell (1968) indicate that there is a widespread need for teaching business managers and other professionals to be more analytical and aware of how they affect others and generally to develop their interpersonal skills. This can be accomplished through gaining a greater insight into one's own personality and increasing awareness of how people behave in different situations, especially in groups (see Cooper 1979). A greater realisation of factors influencing inter- and intra-group situations can help to alleviate many problems and conflicts between people.

Anderson (1973) maintains that the ultimate goal of planning for career growth involves the individual assuming the primary responsibility for pursuing his own career development. This includes:

1. Knowing yourself;

2. Defining goals;

3. Defining actions or events;

4. Establishing priorities;

5. Identifying barriers;

6. Facilitating the career planning process by consciously reviewing and examining your needs and interests, the extent to which your goals are compatible with those of the organisation, your actions and plans, and your priorities.

Many strategies have been used to combat obsolescence by professional bodies, organisations and individuals, but a good deal of research is required to determine their effects on different kinds of managers, in different industries and from different functions.

CONSEQUENCES OF OBSOLESCENCE

What are the consequences for managers if they do not keep their knowledge and skills up-to-date? There are a number of possible outcomes, all of which are not very optimistic for the individual manager, nor indeed for their companies (see Figure 8.1). Some may become so incapable that they are demoted, retired or made redundant. Others may even cause so many problems that whole departments or indeed companies may have to close as a result of incompetence. Hence, this problem of managerial obsolescence has deep-rooted consequences, for not only can it affect the individual, but also his department and company. This in turn will, of course, affect the economy of a country. Therefore, it is crucial at various levels to deal with this problem. Many suggestions have already been alluded to above and in earlier chapters.

Perhaps one of the most difficult aspects of obsolescence is the fact that it often arises over a long period of time in many subtle ways, identified as 'creeping obsolescence' by Mahler (1965). Also, many managers are reluctant to admit to it or face up to its consequences even at a late stage. Earlier work by one of these writers (Jones 1977) found that it was only on becoming redundant that managers often admitted to the fact that they were out-of-date. Perhaps this is not so surprising, for as managers they feel it necessary to project a positive self-image and superior performance and of course in turn, some subordinates help to reinforce this myth for various reasons some of which are not always very healthy. Managers, like others, do not want to 'lose face' in front of subordinates and so will not always admit to lack of knowledge or an inability to do something. They often hide this by becoming angry, aggressive or delegating the problem to someone else. As one manager put it quite succinctly, 'the way to survive is, not to make a decision on anything, and pass all matters which are potentially difficult onto someone else'. The 'buck-passing manager' is well

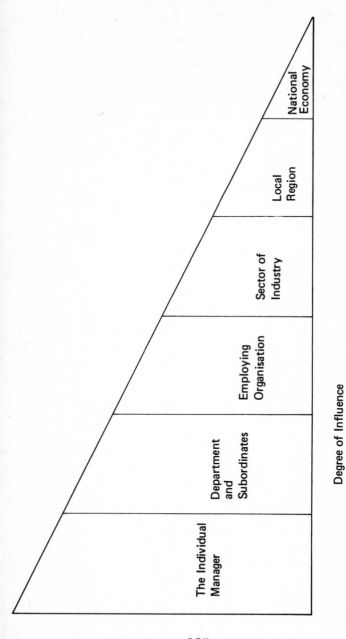

FIGURE 8.1 *Implications of Managerial Obsolescence*

known to most companies but what is not often realised is the harm he can do not only to himself, but also to his subordinates and his company.

Finally, it is the conclusion of the present writers that for obsolescence to be truly and effectively dealt with, it is necessary for the individuals to recognise it in themselves and decide to take action to remedy it. No amount of government, company or other action can hope seriously to affect change unless the individual wants to do something himself. This, coupled with a positive perception of his learning ability and competency to successfully engage in updating experiences, can lead to the final death knell of managerial obsolescence.

CHAPTER 9

Summary and Conclusions

This book was written in order to examine the phenomenon of managerial obsolescence in the context of managers
themselves, their jobs and their organisations. It is based on
an in-depth study of managers carried out between 1977—79
and draws extensively from related work through the use of
a comprehensive literature review of the field. The objective
of the book was to give managers a greater understanding of
obsolescence and its consequences, and to suggest some
strategies that might be useful both for the individual and
his organisation to help cope with or prevent the onset of
managerial obsolescence.

SUMMARY OF SIGNIFICANT VARIABLES IN
RELATION TO MANAGERIAL OBSOLESCENCE

The following variables have been found to be significantly
related to managerial obsolescence (Jones 1979). They are
exemplified here as they relate to the characteristics of high
and low obsolescent managers as found in this study (see
Table 9.1).

Table 9.1 *Profile of High & Low Obsolescent Managers*

Category of Variable	High Obsolescent	Low Obsolescent
Demographic	Younger. Low level of educational attainment. Negative perception of their learning ability. Decline in learning ability in recent years. Do not enjoy learning activities.	Older. High level of educational attainment. Positive perception of their learning ability. Improved learning ability in recent years. Enjoy learning experiences.
Personal	Do not think it is important to keep up-to-date, either for maintaining job or for career development. Not motivated to keep up-to-date. Experience difficulty keeping up with professional literature. Not members of professional association.	Think it is important to keep up-to-date both for maintaining job effectiveness and career development. Motivated to keep up-to-date. Can keep up with professional literature. Members of professional associations.
Career	Likely to work in Production or R & D. Work at junior/middle management level. Will have many years' management experience. Will not have held management posts in other companies. Would not be willing to work outside the country in the future. Will not be contributing much to decision-making. Will not find their jobs challenging. Their skills and abilities will be under-utilised.	Likely to work in Finance or Personnel. Work at senior/board level. Will have less management experience. Will have held management posts in other companies. Willing to work outside the country in the future. Will be contributing a great deal to decision-making. Will find their jobs challenging. Their skills and abilities will be well-utilised.

Organisational	Likely to work in Food, Drink or Tobacco or Printing and Paper companies.	Likely to work in Engineering companies.
	Likely to work for a large company (500+).	Likely to work for a medium or small company.
	Their organisations do not have a policy for career planning.	Their organisations do have a policy for career planning.
	Their organisations do not reward high management performance.	Their organisations do reward high management performance.
	Their organisations do not encourage innovation.	Their organisations do encourage innovation.
	Their organisations are poor at responding to change.	Their organisations are good at responding to change.
	Their superiors will not be interested in their careers.	Their superiors will be interested in their careers.
Personality	More affected by feelings. (factor C).	More emotionally stable.
	More intelligent (factor B).	Less intelligent.
	More suspicious (factor L).	More trusting.
	More humble (factor E).	More assertive.
	More reserved (factor A).	More outgoing.
	More group dependent (factor $Q2$).	More self-sufficient.
	More imaginative (factor M).	More practical.
	More forthright (factor N).	More shrewd.
	Have low motivation to achieve (factor N-Ach).	Have high motivation to achieve.

These results indicate that there are many variables which seem to influence managerial obsolescence, so that any attempt to explain this phenomenon must take acount of all of them. However, the most important variables seem to be managers' perception of their learning ability and the extent to which they enjoy new work-related learning. An examination of the significant variables in the study suggest that the most important group were the personal variables, dealing with managers' learning ability, their perception of the importance of updating and their motivation to keep up-to-date.

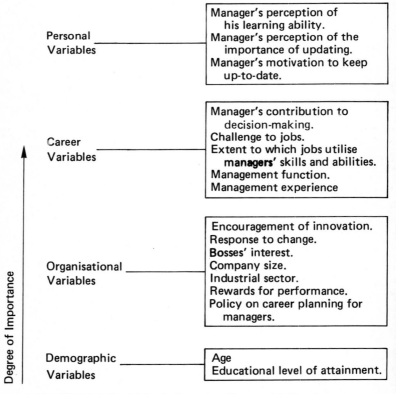

FIGURE 9.1 *Variables Influencing Managerial Obsolescence*

The career variables appear to be next in importance, particularly those relating to decision-making, job challenge and the extent to which managers' jobs utilise their professional skills and abilities.

The third group in terms of explaining managerial obsolescence were the organisational variables, especially those relating to encouragement of innovation, organisations' ability to respond to change and bosses' interest in subordinates' professional growth and development.

The least important group of variables were the demographic ones.

Figure 9.1 illustrates these findings in diagrammatic form.

THE PERSONALITY OF THE OBSOLESCENT MANAGER

The main traits of the obsolescent manager's personality are illustrated in Figure 9.2.

The major differences between high and low obsolescent managers were on entrepreneurial traits, adjustment, level of motivation to achieve and creativity. The remaining two characteristics differed little between the two groups of managers.

Low on entrepreneurial traits

Less well adjusted

Low level of motivation

High on creativity

Above average ability to learn and grow in a new job

Slightly below average mental health

FIGURE 9.2 *Personality of the Obsolescent Manager*

131

These results suggest that the obsolescent manager does not appear to possess the traits traditionally associated with the successful manager. The importance of this finding is the fact that managerial personality may be used as a way of identifying the obsolescent manager from his more up-to-date colleagues.

The following variables were *not* found to be significantly related to managerial obsolescence.

1. Manager's professional/technical qualifications;

2. Number of years in present post or company;

3. Number of management posts held in present company;

4. Previous employment outside the country;

5. Availability or participation in updating activities;

6. Particular areas requiring updating;

7. Whether the employing organisation had a policy for staff updating or not;

8. Influence of organisational policy on staff updating and manager's decision to undertake further education;

9. Whether the employing organisation gave financial aid to its employees for continuing/further education;

10. The type of influences on management training/ development in the employing organisations in recent years;

11. How managers felt about the general question of other managers keeping up-to-date.

SUMMARY DISCUSSION

This final discussion is concerned with the main elements of each of the foregoing chapters. It is presented here in concise form in order to illustrate the interaction of each chapter on the other.

The main conclusions arising from the examination of personal characteristics of managers are that age alone is not a very significant variable in relation to managerial obsolescence.

However, it is important in terms of learning ability. Yet, if managers have a positive perception of their learning ability irrespective of their educational/technical qualifications, they can and will keep up-to-date. If on the other hand they have a poor perception of their learning ability, this is usually associated with a negative attitude to updating and hence a ready recipe for obsolescence. Managers' work experience was found to be very important in keeping them up-to-date. It is necessary for managers at all levels to have challenging and worthwhile work which provides them with plenty of stimulation and job satisfaction. The absence of this can lead to mobility which is not necessarily a panacea and in fact can often be used as an escape rather than for professional growth and development. Membership of professional associations is important for managers because of the benefits derived from attending seminars, meetings etc. and the opportunity they provide for colleagues to discuss common problems and experiences.

The most important and helpful updating activities that managers engaged in were educational courses in their own time and on-the-job problem-solving. The most commonly engaged in activities are however, reading work-related books and journals, on-the-job problem-solving and attending seminars and conferences.

In terms of personality variables, the results show that a positive self-concept is an important trait of managers who are up-to-date.

Those with a high self-esteem are more likely to ward off obsolescence because they are independent, confident and willing to take risks in order to progress their careers. Managers who were capable of coping with change were found to be less vulnerable to obsolescence because they were open to new ideas, flexible, risk takers and interested in keeping up-to-date. Intelligence appears to be a factor influencing susceptibility to obsolescence. Those with a high intellectual ability tend to pursue updating activities more readily than those with lower ability.

Achievement motivation has been found to be a major factor influencing vulnerability to obsolescence. Managers with high achievement needs tend to set more demanding goals for themselves, expend larger amounts of energy trying to achieve them, and use their initiative more than those with lower achievement needs. Finally, it has been found that 'cosmopolitan' managers are less likely to become out-of-date than 'local' managers, because they are more determined to keep abreast of changes and developments in their particular profession.

In terms of our study of managers, the high obsolescence group of managers were similar to the low obsolescence group in terms of mental health, but slightly higher in terms of ability to learn and capacity to grow in a new job, and creativity. But, they were less entrepreneurial, less well adjusted and had a lower level of motivation to achieve than the low obsolescence group of managers.

In relation to career characteristics, a number of points are worth noting. The first of these is that different functions appear to be more or less susceptible to obsolescence, with Finance and Personnel being less than Production and R & D. The reason for this seems to be related to the length of time managers engage in study during their careers. The former two groups appear to study longer into their careers than the latter groups who may be better qualified academically, but are likely to have completed their formal studies prior to embarking on their careers.

The hierarchical level of managers seems to influence their level of obsolescence, but not in any clearcut fashion. Many junior/middle managers become obsolescent because of unchallenging work or frustration caused by lack of promotion. They may also experience mis-utilisation or under-utilisation of their knowledge and skills. Senior managers on the other hand may be kept up-to-date because of the stimulating nature of their work and their willingness to take risks, which of course may relate to why they are senior managers in the first place.

Managers' decision-making responsibilities and job challenge appear to be related. Those who are actively engaged in functional and company decision-making, in other words, those who are listened to, seem to be the most likely to be kept up-to-date. Managers with challenging jobs which utilise their professional skills and abilities tend to find it easier to keep up-to-date than others. These findings emphasise the importance of challenging job assignments, whatever the function or level in the hierarchy in maintaining updatedness.

In relation to supervisory behaviour, the conclusions are that although supervisors should encourage their subordinates to engage in updating activities and help to provide the necessary resources to do so, it is still very much up to the individual manager to take responsibility for his own updating. It has been found that no matter what a supervisor may or may not do, if an individual manager is determined to keep up-to-date he will do so, for ultimately he alone has to participate in, and derive benefit from, updating activities. If he neglects this, he will undoubtedly become a victim of managerial obsolescence.

From an organisational viewpoint, it was found that different industrial sectors seem to experience managerial obsolescence to varying degrees. This is related to the type of technology present in the industry and the rate of change within that technology. Managers in smaller companies appear to be less prone to obsolescence than their counterparts in larger (500+) companies. This is related to the fact that they have to deal with all aspects of their function, while the others generally tend to specialise in narrow aspects of their functions and hence do not keep up-to-date quite so readily from a functional viewpoint.

The presence or absence of a company policy on updating or career planning does not seem seriously to affect managerial obsolescence, for as mentioned in previous chapters it is the manager himself who must take responsibility for his own updating. However, this is not to say that organisations can ignore the question, for it is still beneficial if they encourage their managers to keep abreast of change and provide the facilities to do so. Career planning is important in order to ensure that managers will have challenging job assignments throughout their careers and that their knowledge and skills will not go into decline through lack of use.

Rewards for high management performance can provide effective incentives for managers to keep up-to-date, but it is important that these rewards be recognised by managers and be related to the jobs they do.

Encouragement of innovation can help to ensure that managers utilise their creative potential to cope with the ever-changing demands of their jobs. This in turn can have a beneficial effect on everyday problem-solving which facilitates managers' professional growth and development.

Organisational response to change has been found to affect managerial obsolescence, for if a company is good at responding to change, this influences the willingness or attitude of managers towards engaging in updating activities. It also affects and influences the degree of job challenge available for managers which, as pointed out above, is related to how up-to-date their knowledge is.

In terms of coping with or preventing the onset of managerial obsolescence, the following are of note. From the individual's viewpoint it is essential that managers engage in continuous learning activities whether formal or informal. This involves *learning to learn* so that they can derive benefit from new job experiences. It also involves taking responsibility for one's own learning and not waiting for others to make suggestions or provide opportunities. The up-to-date manager is one who takes the initiative whatever the situation and strives to keep abreast of new knowledge and skills as related to his discipline.

From an organisational standpoint many approaches can be used to help cope with or prevent the onset of managerial obsolescence. These include promotion, demotion, job rotation, special assignments, on-the-job training, job enrichment, career planning, industrial encouragement of innovation, rewards for high performance and incentives to engage in updating activities.

Management development generally, and those engaged in the provision of same in particular, need to examine closely both the content and methodologies employed in their programmes. Many managers express a need for further input on such topics as Finance and Personnel, but these are not necessarily related to the traditional inputs provided under these broad headings. Many non-financial managers need a greater understanding of Finance, but this of necessity must be non-technical, for otherwise it will not be understood. In the area of Personnel, the greatest need appears to be in the field of interpersonal communications, man-management and motivation, rather than the technical aspects of the discipline. Managers indicate that their greatest learning often comes from on-the-job problem-solving which, by its very nature, is experiential and informal. This suggests that greater use could be made of this form of learning than exposing managers to numerous lectures and highly structured learning experiences. Professional associations also have a role to play in providing a service to their members which will help them to keep up-to-date with changes in their disciplines.

The value of formal training programmes was discussed earlier and the relative cost of same in relation to the value

137

derived from them. It seems that a great deal of money is spent each year on courses which give little value either to the individual participant or his employing organisation. Perhaps what is often missing is the careful identification of managers' training needs prior to sending them on formal courses or designing suitable in-company courses. A further aspect of this is that often managers are sent on courses for the wrong reasons which in turn mitigates against any possibility of successful learning.

This chapter also discusses why managers go on courses; these are often unrelated to such variables as seeking academic qualifications and more to the desire to do their present job better. It has also been found that those who attend courses are often the best, while those who are least likely to attend courses need them the most. Some managers only attend courses when they see that there is a payoff at the end, but provision of educational assistance funds was not seen as a motivating factor for many.

Finally, the effects of managerial obsolescence can be felt at many levels, firstly by the individual manager who may no longer be capable of carrying out his duties as efficiently or effectively as before. Secondly, by his department or section which may suffer as a result of this individual incompetency which in turn will affect the overall company. Then collectively, companies who are having difficulties due to managerial obsolescence will affect the economy of a country. This may sound somewhat alarmist, but if one examines the logic of it, it is understandable. Because of this it is necessary to tackle managerial obsolescence at a variety of levels from governmental to organisational to individual. However, it is the conclusion of these writers that it is the individual manager who is the key to the successful handling of the problem for he must ultimately take the major responsibility for his own updating.

CONCLUSIONS

The main conclusions drawn from our study of managerial obsolescence are as follows:

1. There are a wide variety of variables which are significantly related to managerial obsolescence;

2. Managerial obsolescence is influenced both by the functions managers work in and their level in the hierarchy;

3. The type of industry and size of company managers work in affect their level of obsolescence;

4. Managerial obsolescence is best studied by examining the interactive effects of different variables rather than by treating them individually;

5. In terms of the different sets of variables examined in this study, their order of importance in relation to managerial obsolescence was Personal, Career, Organisational and Demographic;

6. There are significant differences in personality between managers who rate themselves highly obsolescent and those who rate themselves up-to-date;

7. The main implications of the results of our study for managers are that they develop a positive attitude to learning and engage in continuous learning activities, both formal and informal. Managers must also take responsibility for their own updating and not rely on their superiors or their organisations to do it for them;

8. The implications of the results for organisations are

that they take an active interest in managers and their careers, recognise functional differences and provide interesting and challenging work assignments which will utilise managers' professional skills and abilities. Organisations should also reward high management performance and carry out long-term career planning for their staff. They should be aware of change and capable of responding to it. Furthermore, it is important for all managers to take an active interest in their subordinates' growth and development.

APPENDIX 1

Questionnaires

	Column
	Col. 1 = 1

1. ⬜⬜⬜⬜⬜⬜⬜⬜⬜⬜⬜   2–12

For questions 2–11 please tick box(es) or insert number where appropriate.

2. In which of the following functions is your present post?   13

Finance ☐ 1

Personnel ☐ 2

Production ☐ 3

Research and Development ☐ 4

Other (Please Specify) ☐ 5

3. Which of these best describes your
   present post?   14

    Board Level   ☐ 1

    Senior Manager   ☐ 2

    Middle Manager   ☐ 3

    Junior Manager   ☐ 4

4. For how many years have
   you held this post?   ☐☐   15—16

5. How many management
   posts (including present post)
   have you held in your
   present company?   ☐☐   17—18

6. For how many years have
   you worked for your present
   company?   ☐☐   19—20

7. In your work career to date,
   how many years' management
   experience do you have?   ☐☐   21—22

8. In how many other
   companies have you
   held management
   posts?   ☐☐   23—24

9. Have you ever held   Yes ☐ 1   25
   permanent employment
   outside this country?   No ☐ 2

10. If 'Yes' was it at a
management level?

Yes ☐ 1   26

No ☐ 2

Not Applicable ☐ 3

11. Whether or not you
have worked outside
this country, would you
be willing to consider
doing so in the future?

Yes ☐ 1   27

No ☐ 2

In all questions with a rating scale such as this

   High   5 4 3 2 1   *Low*

please respond by circling appropriate number.

12. In general, how would you rate your
present ability to learn new work-related
knowledge/skill? (Please circle appropriate
number.)   28

High   5 4 3 2 1   Low

13. To what extent has your ability to learn
changed in the past five years?   29

Improved   5 4 3 2 1   Disimproved

14. How much do you enjoy new work-
related learning?   30

Very much   5 4 3 2 1   Very little

15. How relevant do you consider your
present professional knowledge (as
opposed to skill) for your current job?   31

Very
Relevant   5 4 3 2 1   Not
Relevant

143

16. How would you rate this knowledge in relation to your current job? | 32

In Excess
of Job   5 4 3 2 1   Below
Demands   Job
                             Demands

17. How relevant do you consider your present skills for your current job? | 33

Very   5 4 3 2 1   Not
Relevant   Relevant

18. How would you rate these skills in relation to the demands of your current job? | 34

In Excess
of Job   5 4 3 2 1   Below
Demands   Job
                             Demands

For the following list of updating activities:

19. In Column A please indicate those that have been available to you in the past 2 years.

20. In Column B please indicate those that you have availed yourself of in the past 2 years.

21. Of those you have availed yourself of, please rank in Column C the four (1—4) that you have found most effective during the past 2 years.

                                    Responses
                                  A   B   C

In-company training   ☐   ☐   ☐ | 35—37
programme

Job-related external training programmes	☐	☐	☐	38—40
Secondment to other organisation	☐	☐	☐	41—43
Job rotation within own organisation	☐	☐	☐	44—46
Educational leave	☐	☐	☐	47—49
On-the-job problem-solving	☐	☐	☐	50—52
Attendance at professional society meetings	☐	☐	☐	53—55
Seminars/conferences	☐	☐	☐	56—58
Reading work-related books	☐	☐	☐	59—61
Reading work-related journals	☐	☐	☐	62—64
Educational programmes in your own time (Please Specify)	☐	☐	☐	65—67
Other (Please Specify)	☐	☐	☐	68—70

22. How important have your updating activities been for maintaining effectiveness in your present job?   71

Very   5 4 3 2 1   Not Very
Important   Important

23. How important have your updating activities been for your own career development?   72

Very   5 4 3 2 1   Not Very
Important   Important

24. How would you rate your present level of motivation to keep up-to-date? 73

Very High 5 4 3 2 1 Very Low

25. How has this changed over the past 5 years? 74

Increased 5 4 3 2 1 Decreased

26. How challenging generally do you find your job assignments? 75

Very 5 4 3 2 1 Not at all

27. How employable do you think your skills are within other organisations? 76

Very 5 4 3 2 1 Not at all

Column
1 = 2
Dup. 2–12

28. In what areas, if any, do you feel you could benefit from updating? 13–14

_____

_____

_____

29. To what extent do you find it difficult to keep up-to-date with professional literature in your field? 15

Very Difficult 5 4 3 2 1 Not Difficult

146

Please comment on the nature of the difficulty if any.

16—17

_____

_____

_____

30. Does your organisation have a policy in relation to continuing/ further education and training for its employees?

Yes ☐ 1

No ☐ 2

Don't ☐ 3
Know

18

If 'Yes' please describe it briefly

19—20

_____

31. To what extent are your personal decisions to undertake further education influenced by your organisation's policy?

Very much 5 4 3 2 1   Not at all
influenced   influenced

21

32. Does your organisation give financial aid to its employees for continuing/further education?

Yes ☐ 1

No ☐ 2

Don't ☐ 3
Know

22

33. To what extent does your organisation carry out long-range career planning for its management staff?

Very much 5 4 3 2 1   Not at all

23

34. To what extent is high manager perform-   24
ance rewarded by your organisation?

Very much   5 4 3 2 1   Not at all

35. In general how much influence would   25—26
you say you have in important decisions
taken:

(a) In your own functional area?

Very much   5 4 3 2 1   Not at all

(b) In your company?

Very much   5 4 3 2 1   Not at all

36. To what extent does your present job   27
utilise your professional skills/abilities?

Very much   5 4 3 2 1   Not at all

37. To what extent does your organisation   28
encourage managers to be innovative?

Very much   5 4 3 2 1   Not at all

38. In your opinion, how interested is your   29
immediate boss in your growth and
development as a professional i.e. not
only in relation to your job?

Very much   5 4 3 2 1   Not at all

39. Which of the following comes closest to   30
describing your immediate boss's attitude/
approach to keeping his subordinates
professionally up-to-date (we know that
none of these is likely to describe it
accurately, but please select the one that
most closely fits)?

A ☐

Is very sensitive to education/
training needs of subordinates.
Tries to create new opportunities
in addition to existing ones, and
to provide novel and interesting
ways for subordinates to keep
professionally up-to-date.

B ☐

Conceives development as a
responsibility of the subordinate.
Neither stimulates subordinates
to pursue additional knowledge,
nor initiates continuing education/
training on their behalf.

C ☐

Conceives of his job as implementing
general organisation training
policies and encouraging subordinates
to use existing resources for self-
development.

D ☐

None of above (Please give brief
description) _____

40. To what extent do you regard your   31
    company as capable of responding to
    change?

    Very   5 4 3 2 1   Not at all

41. What have been major influences on   32—33
    management training/development in
    your organisation?

42. Do you have any comments regarding the general question of managers keeping up-to-date?   34—35

Biographical Data:
43. Age   Under 35   ☐ 1   36

         35—49 years   ☐ 2

         50 + years   ☐ 3

44. *Marital Status:*   37

         Married   ☐ 1

         Single   ☐ 2

         Widowed/ Separated   ☐ 3

45. Academic Qualification(s):   38—39

         Primary Certificate   ☐ 01

         Inter/Group Certificate   ☐ 02

         Leaving Certificate or Equivalent   ☐ 03

         Third Level Qualification(s)   ☐ 04

Please list (Third level only)

46. All other Professional/Technical
    Qualification(s)
    Please list: 40—41

    _____

    _____

    _____

47. Please list the professional associations
    (if any) to which you belong. Indicate:

    (1) the approximate length of member-
    ship and
    (2) the degree of your activity in each
    association as follows:

                1 = Inactive
                2 = Relatively Inactive
                3 = Moderately Active
                4 = Active

Name of Professional Association	Approx. Duration of Membership No. of Yrs	Level of Activity (Circle appropriate no.)	
_____	☐☐	4 3 2 1	42—46
_____	☐☐	4 3 2 1	47—51
_____	☐☐	4 3 2 1	52—56
_____	☐☐	4 3 2 1	57—61

THANK YOU FOR YOUR CO-OPERATION

ACHIEVEMENT MOTIVATION QUESTIONNAIRE

N-Ach Scale (Smith, 1973)

Name......................... Sex ....

Date .... Age ....

INSTRUCTIONS

Read each of the following statements. If you think that it is true underline the TRUE. If you think that it is false underline the FALSE.

Please do not miss out any statements. Even though it may be difficult, you must decide one way or the other.

1.	I am *not* clear about the instructions for this test	TRUE	FALSE
2.	When I was young I enjoyed the feeling of accomplishment after I had done something well	TRUE	FALSE
3.	The feeling of a job well done is a great satisfaction	TRUE	FALSE
4.	I don't think I'm a good trier	TRUE	FALSE
5.	I would sooner admire a winner than win myself	TRUE	FALSE
6.	If it's worth doing, it's worth doing well	TRUE	FALSE
7.	Failure is no sin	TRUE	FALSE
8.	Incentives do more harm than good	TRUE	FALSE
9.	In an unknown situation it doesn't pay to be pessimistic	TRUE	FALSE
10.	I dislike red tape	TRUE	FALSE
11.	I work best when I have a job that I like	TRUE	FALSE

12.	It's never best to set one's own challenges	TRUE	FALSE
13.	I don't care what others do, I go my own way	TRUE	FALSE
14.	Even a good poker player can't do much with a poor hand	TRUE	FALSE
15.	Modern life isn't too competitive	TRUE	FALSE
16.	You can try too hard sometimes, it's best to let the world drift by	TRUE	FALSE
17.	Most people want success because it brings respect	TRUE	FALSE

Please check back to see that you haven't missed any out.

APPENDIX 2

Tables

Table A.1 *Distribution of the Sample by Professional Association Membership*

Name of Association	N*	%
Association of Chartered Accountants	47	21.8
Assoc. of Cost & Mgt. Accountants	34	15.7
Inst. of Personnel Management	29	13.4
Irish Management Institute	19	8.8
Irish Inst. of Training Managers	19	8.8
Institute of Industrial Engineers	17	7.9
Irish Engineering Industries	13	6.0
Irish Creamery Managers' Assoc.	10	4.6
Irish Inst. of Secretaries & Admins.	8	3.7
Institute of Food Technology	7	3.2
Institute of Dairy Technology	5	2.3
Irish Institute of Marketing	4	1.9
Institute of Bankers	3	1.4
Institute of Financial Executives	3	1.4
Institute of Materials Handling	3	1.4
Institute of Printers	2	0.9
Institute of Production Managers	2	0.9
Institute of Packaging	2	0.9
Others	111	51.4

Total number of managers: 216, with 338 memberships in professional associations.

109 Missing Cases

*Numbers not mutually exclusive.

154

Table A.2 *Relationship between Demographic Variables and Obsolescence Variables*

Hypothesis Variables		Relevance of knowledge		Adequacy of knowledge		Relevance of skill		Adequacy of skill		Employability of skill		Comments
		x^2	p	x^2	p	x^2	p	x^2	p	x^2	p	
1.	Age	3.847	0.697	17.950	0.025*	4.712	0.581	3.345	0.911	13.532	0.095**	Age is significantly related to adequacy of knowledge and employability of skills.
2.	First and Second Level Education.	16.128	0.444	27.361	0.125	4.989	0.0958	30.137	0.068**	6.187	0.999	First and Second level of educational attainment is significantly related to adequacy of skills.
	Third Level Education.	18.395	0.916	36.533	0.397	25.252	0.236	26.668	0.843	28.388	0.778	Third level is not significantly related to any of the obsolescence variables.
3.	Professional /Technical Qualifications.	10.918	0.998	29.968	0.709	17.913	0.655	42.505	0.179	26.346	0.854	Professional/ technical qualifications are not significantly related to any of the obsolescence variables.

* **Significantly related at 0.05 level.**
** **Significantly related at 0.09 level.**

Table A.3 *Relationship between Personal Variables and Obsolescence Variables*

Hypothesis	Variables	Relevance of knowledge		Adequacy of knowledge		Relevance of skill		Adequacy of skill		Employability of skill		Comments
		r	p	r	p	r	p	r	p	r	p	
1.	Ability to learn new work-related knowledge and skills.	0.180	0.001*	0.138	0.007*	0.221	0.001*	0.187	0.001*	0.302	0.001*	Learning ability is significantly related to all obsolescence variables.
	Change in learning ability in recent years.	0.073	0.096**	0.153	0.003*	0.205	0.001*	0.257	0.001*	0.175	0.001*	Change in learning ability is significantly related to all obsolescence variables.
	Enjoyment of learning.	0.115	0.020*	0.097	0.040*	0.213	0.001*	0.121	0.015*	0.158	0.002*	Enjoyment of learning is significantly related to all obsolescence variables.
2.	Importance of updating for maintaining job effectiveness.	0.143	0.006*	0.064	0.129	0.091	0.055**	−0.026	0.322	0.184	0.001*	Importance of updating for job effectiveness is significantly related to relevance of knowledge and skills, and employability of skills.
	Importance of updating for career development.	0.164	0.002*	0.053	0.170	0.092	0.048*	−0.016	0.385	0.253	0.001*	Importance of updating for career development is significantly related

	x^2	p	x^2	p	x^2	p	x^2	p	x^2	p	
Motivation to update.	0.150	0.004*	0.052	0.175	0.208	0.001*	0.077	0.086**	0.380	0.001*	Motivation to update is significantly related to all obsolescence variables, except adequacy of knowledge. to relevance of knowledge and skills, and employability of skills.
Change in motivation to update in recent years.	0.058	0.151	0.055	0.162	0.152	0.003*	0.075	0.089**	0.138	0.007*	Change in motivation to update is significantly related to relevance, adequacy and employability of skills.
3. Participation in updating activities.	Chi square tests were carried out on all 12 activities separately, but none of the values was significant.										Participation in updating activities is not significantly related to any of the obsolescence variables.
4. Membership of Professional Association.	66.094	0.376	120.486	0.005**	201.693	0.001**	217.141	0.001**	91.849	0.264	Membership of Professional Associations is significantly related to adequacy of knowledge, and relevance and adequacy of skill.

* Significantly related at 0.05 level.
** Significantly related at 0.09 level.

157

Table A.4 *Relationship between Career Variables and Obsolescence Variables*

Hypothesis	Variables	Relevance of knowledge		Adequacy of knowledge		Relevance of skill		Adequacy of skill		Employability of skill		Comments
		x^2	p	x^2	p	x^2	p	x^2	p	x^2	p	
1.	Management Function.	12.435	0.646	66.687	0.001*	18.367	0.244	34.649	0.022*	46.966	0.001*	Management function is significantly related to adequacy of knowledge and skill and employability of skills.
2.	Hierarchical Level.	13.699	0.320	19.717	0.233	12.174	0.432	13.885	0.607	25.684	0.059*	Hierarchical level is significantly related to employability of skill.
		r	p	r	p	r	p	r	p	r	p	
3.	Management Experience.	0.075	0.091**	0.099	0.038*	−0.056	0.460	−0.057	0.153	−0.138	0.006*	Management experience is significantly related to relevance and adequacy of knowledge and negatively related to employability of skills.

158

4.	Functional decision-making.	0.189 0.001*	−0.033 0.278	0.226 0.001*	0.060 0.143	0.190 0.001*	Functional decision-making is significantly related to relevance of knowledge and skill and employability of skill.
	Company decision-making.	0.251 0.001*	0.151 0.003*	0.179 0.001*	0.133 0.009*	0.210 0.001*	Company decision-making is significantly related to all obsolescence variables.
5.	Challenge of job.	0.258 0.001*	−0.025 0.328	0.281 0.001*	0.009 0.439	0.227 0.001*	Challenge of job is significantly related to relevance of knowledge and skills, and employability of skills.
	Extent to which job utilises managers' skills and abilities.	0.362 0.001*	−0.058 0.150	0.332 0.001*	−0.071 0.101	0.296 0.001*	Utilisation of managers skills and abilities is significantly related to relevance of knowledge and skills and employability of skills.

6.						
Management experience in other companies	−0.021 0.352	−0.026 0.321	0.012 0.414	0.028 0.307	−0.184 0.001*	Management experience is significantly negatively related to employability of skills.
Previously worked outside Ireland	−0.043 0.222	0.035 0.264	0.024 0.333	−0.039 0.240	−0.032 0.286	Overseas experience is not significantly related to obsolescence variables.
At management level.	0.071 0.101	0.026 0.321	−0.022 0.348	−0.022 0.349	−0.006 0.457	Overseas experience at management level is not significantly related to obsolescence variables.
Willingness to work outside Ireland in the future.	−0.024 0.336	0.042 0.224	0.024 0.330	−0.019 0.366	−0.111 0.023	Willingness to work outside Ireland is significantly related to employability of skills.

* Significantly related at 0.05 level.
** Significantly related at 0.09 level.

Table A.5 *Relationship between Organisational Variables with Obsolescence Variables*

Hypothesis	Variables	Relevance of knowledge		Adequacy of knowledge		Relevance of skill		Adequacy of skill		Employability of skill		Comments
		x^2	p	x^2	p	x^2	p	x^2	p	x^2	p	
1.	Industrial Sector	8.783	0.186	22.801	0.004*	4.511	0.608	9.617	0.293	22.181	0.005*	Industrial Sector is significantly related to adequacy of knowledge and employability of skills.
		r	p	r	p	r	p	r	p	r	p	
2.	Company Size	−0.075	0.089**	−0.084	0.067**	−0.030	0.293	−0.142	0.005	−0.009	0.433	Company size is significantly negatively related to relevance of knowledge and adequacy of knowledge and skills.
3.	Organisation's Policy for Staff up-dating	−0.020	0.358	0.044	0.216	0.031	0.288	0.039	0.244	−0.049	0.191	There is not a significant relationship between whether a company has policy for staff updating and obsolescence.

161

4.	Companies carrying out long-range planning for management staff	0.054 0.170	0.043 0.219	−0.060 0.142	−0.027 0.315	0.134 0.008**	Long-range career planning for management staff is significantly related to employability of skills.
5.	Rewards for high management performance	0.058 0.150	0.076 0.089**	0.063 0.129	0.050 0.189	0.157 0.003*	Rewards for high management performance are significantly related to adequacy of knowledge and employability of skills.
6.	Encouragement of innovation	0.195 0.001*	0.023 0.339	0.137 0.007*	0.022 0.347	0.180 0.001*	Encouragement of innovation is significantly related to relevance of knowledge and skills, and employability of skills.

No.	Variable						Interpretation
7.	Organisation's response to change.	0.138 0.007*	0.055 0.165	0.133 0.009*	0.030 0.300	0.185 0.001*	Organisation's response to change is significantly related to relevance of knowledge and skills, and employability of skills.
8.	Bosses' interest in subordinates' growth and development as professionals	0.099 0.038*	0.015 0.397	0.087 0.060**	0.008 0.446	0.146 0.004*	Bosses' interest in subordinates' growth and development is significantly related to relevance of knowledge and skills, and employability of skills.

* Significantly related at 0.05 level
** Significantly related at 0.09 level

References

Anderson, S.D. (1973), Planning for career growth, *Personnel Journal*, Vol. 52(5), pp. 357–362.

Ansoff, H.I. (1973), The next twenty years in management education, in Fussler, H.H., Jenck, J.E. and Swanson, D.R. (eds), *Implications for Libraries and Library Schools*, University of Chicago, Graduate School of Library Science, 36th Annual Conference, pp. 13–48.

Argyris, C. (1964), *Integrating the Individual and the Organisation*, John Wiley.

Argyris, C. (1965), *Organisation and Innovation*, Irwin-Dorsey.

Atkinson, J.S. and Feather, N.T. (1966), *A Theory of Achievement Motivation*, John Wiley.

Barrett, G.V., Bass, B.M. and Miller, J.A. (1971), Combating obsolescence using perceived discrepancies in job expectations of research managers and scientists, in Dubin, S.S. (ed.), *Professional Obsolescence*, English University Press, pp. 59–71.

Bass, B.M. (1970), The task-oriented manager, in Bass, B.M., Cooper, R. and Hass, J.A. (eds), *Managing for Accomplishment*, Heath, pp. 5–12.

Belbin, E. (1964), *Training the Adult Worker*, Problems of Progress in Industry, No. 15, HMSO, London.

Belbin, E. (1969), *Older Adults in Training*, Association of Technical Institutions, Seminar Meeting, Eastbourne, 5th–6th June.

Belbin, E. and Downs, S. (1966), Teaching paired associates: the problem of age, *Occupational Psychology*, Vol. 40(1), pp. 67–74.

Belbin, E. and Belbin, R.M. (1972), *Problems in Adult Retraining*, Heinemann.

Belbin, R.M. (1965), *Training Methods for Older Workers*, OECD, Paris.

Benjamin, D.R. (1967), *A Thirty-One-Year Longitudinal Study of Engineering Students*, Doctoral dissertation, Purdue University, Indiana.

Bennett, J.B. and Weiher, R.L. (1972), The well-read manager, *Harvard Business Review*, Vol. 50(4), pp. 134–146.

Berkwitt, G.J. (1972), Management — sitting on a time bomb, *Duns*, Vol. 100(1).

Blood, M.R. and Hulin, C.L. (1967), Alienation, environmental characteristics, and worker responses, *Journal of Applied Psychology*, Vol. 51(2), pp. 284–290.

Botwinick, J., Brinley, J.F. and Robbin, J.S. (1958), The interaction effects on perceptual difficulty and stimulus exposure time of age differences in speed and accuracy response, *Gerontologia*, Vol. 2(1), pp. 1–5.

Botwinick, J. (1966), Cautiousness in advanced age, *Journal of Gerontology*, Vol. 21(3), pp. 347–353.

Boxer, P. (1975), Towards a framework of course design for developing managers, London Graduate School of Business Studies (unpublished paper).

Brady, R.H. (1967), Computers in top level decision-making, *Harvard Business Review*, Vol. 45(4), pp. 67–76.

Brunning, R.H., Holzbauer, I. and Kimberlin, C. (1975), Age, word imagery and delay: internal effects on short-term and long-term retention, *Journal of Gerontology*, Vol. 22(3), pp. 312–318.

Buck, V. (1972), *Working Under Pressure*. Staples Press, London.

Burack, E.H. and Pati, G.C. (1970a), Technology and managerial obsolescence, *MSU Business Topics*, Vol. 18(2), pp. 49–56.

Burack, E.H. and Pati, G.C. (1970b), Every company's problem—managerial obsolescence, *Personnel*, Vol. 2.

Burgoyne, J. and Stuart, R. (1978), Teaching and learning methods in management development, *Personnel Review*, Vol. 7(1), pp. 53–58.

Buzan, T. (1977), The potential to learn, *BACIE Journal*, Vol. 31(9).

Cattell, R.B., Eber, H.W. and Tatsuoka, N.M. (1970), *Handbook for the Sixteen Personality Factor Questionnaire (16PF)*, NFER Publishing, Windsor, UK.

Chamberlain, A. (1974), *An Executive Odyssey: Looking for a Job at Fifty-five*, Fortune.

Chambers, J.A. (1964), Relating personality and biographical factors to scientific creativity, *Psychological Monographs*, Vol. 78, (No. 7, Serial Whole Number 584).

Chown, S., Belbin, E. and Downs, S. (1967), Programmed instruction as a method of teaching paired associates to older learners, *Journal of Gerontology*, Vol. 22(2), pp. 212–219.

Committee on Utilisation of Scientific and Engineering Manpower (1964), *Towards Better Utilisation of Scientific and Engineering Talent: A Programme for Action*, National Academy of Sciences, Washington DC.

165

Connor, S.R. and Fielden, J.S. (1973), Rx for managerial shelf sitters, *Harvard Business Review*, Vol. 51(6), pp. 113–120.

Cooper, C.L. (1973), *Group Training for Individual and Organisational Development*, S. Karger, Basle.

Cooper, C.L. (1975), *Developing Social Skills in Managers: Advances in Group Training Education*, Macmillan Press.

Cooper, C.L. (1979), *Learning from Others in Groups*, Associated Business Press, London.

Craik, F.I.M. (1969), Applications of signal detection theory to studies of ageing, in Welford, A.T. and Birren, J.E. (eds), *Decision-making and Age*, S. Karger, Basle.

Crossman, E.R.F.W. and Szafran, J. (1956), Changes with age in the speed of information — intake and discrimination, *Experientia Supplements*, Vol. 4.

Crossman, E.R.F.W. (1960), *Automation and Skill Problems of Progress in Industry*, HMSO, London, pp. 4–5, 35, 38, 42–43.

Dalton, G.W. and Thompson, P.H. (1971), Accelerating obsolescence of older engineers, *Harvard Business Review*, Vol. 49(5), pp. 57–67.

Dalton, G.W., Thompson, P.H. and Price, A.L. (1977), *The Four Stages of Professional Careers — A New Look at Performance by Professionals. Organisation Dynamics*, AMACON, New York, pp. 19–42.

Daniel, W.W. (1970), Strategies for displaced employees, Political and Economic Planning Broadsheet 38, No. 517, London.

Daniel, W.W. (1972), What interests a worker?, *New Society*, 23, March.

Donaldson, J. and Gowler, D. (1975), Prerogatives, participation and managerial stress, in Gowler, D. and Legge, K. (eds), *Managerial Stress*, Gower Press.

Drucker, P.F. (1969), *The Age of Discontinuity*, Harper and Row.

Drucker, P.F. (1971), Peter Drucker attacks: our top-heavy corporations, *Duns*, Vol. 97(4).

Dubin, S.S. and Marlow, H. Le Roy (1965), *A Survey of Continuing Professional Education for Engineers in Pennsylvania*, Department of Planning Studies, Continuing Education, The Pennsylvania State University.

Dubin, S.S., Alderman, E. and Marlow, H. Le Roy (1967), *Managerial and Supervisory Education Needs of Businesses and Industry in Pennsylvania*, Department of Planning Studies, Continuing Education, The Pennsylvania State University.

Dubin, S.S. (1972), *Professional Obsolescence*, English University Press, New York.

Dunnette, M.G. and Campbell, J.P. (1968), Laboratory education: impact on people and organisations, *Industrial Relations*, October, Vol. 8(1), pp. 1–27.

Einstein, K. (1972), Screening executives: the guy who just slipped by, *Management Review*, Vol. 61(7), pp. 26–32.

Evan, W.M. (1963), The Problem of Obsolescence of Knowledge, IEEE Transactions in Engineering Management, EM-10, pp. 29–31.

Farris, G.F. (1973), Motivating R & D performance in a stable organisation, *Research Management*, Vol. 16(5), pp. 22—27.

Ferdinand, N. (1966), On the obsolescence of scientists and engineers, *American Scientists*, Vol. 54.

Ford Foundation Report (1967), *Establishment of Domestic Satellite Facilities by Non-Governmental Entities*, New York, Vol. 1.

Fox, E.H. (1965), Personal obsolescence — a personal challenge, *The Personnel Administration*, Vol. 28(3).

French, J.R.P. and Caplan, R.D. (1970), Psychological factors in coronary heart disease, *Industrial Medicine*, Vol. 39, pp. 383—97.

French, J.R.P. and Caplan, R.D. (1973), Organisational stress and individual strain, in Marrow (ed.), *The Failure of Success*, AMACON, New York.

Gaudet, F.J. and Carli, A.R. (1957), Why executives fail, *Personnel Psychology*, Vol. 10(1), pp. 7—21.

George, J.L. and Dubin, S.S. (1972), *Continuing Education Needs of National Research Managers and Scientists*, Department of Planning Studies, Continuing Education, The Pennsylvania State University.

Glaser, B.G. (1963), *Organisational Scientists: Their Professional Careers*, Bobbs-Merrill.

Gould, R. (1975), Adult life stages — growth towards self-tolerance, *Psychology Today*, February.

Gregory, R.L. (1974), *Concepts and Mechanisms of Perception*, Charles Scribner's Sons.

Haas, F.C. (1968), *Executive Obsolescence*, AMA Research Study 90, New York.

Hall, D.T. (1971), Potential for career growth, *Personnel Administration*, Vol. 34(3), pp. 18—30.

Hanson, M.C. (1977), Career development responsibilities of managers, *Personnel Journal*, Vol. 56(9), pp. 443—445.

Hartley, J.F. (1978), *An Investigation of Psychological Aspects of Managerial Unemployment*, Doctoral dissertation, UMIST.

Hartston, W.R. and Mottram, R.D. (1975), *Personality Profiles of Managers: A Study of Occupational Differences*, Industrial Training Research Unit Publication SL9, Cambridge, UK.

Hertzberg, F., Mausner, B. and Synderman, B. (1959), *The Motivation to Work*, John Wiley.

Hesseling, P. (1971), Factors in the organisation climate which stimulate innovation in professional knowledge and skills, in Dubin, S.S. (ed.), *Professional Obsolescence*, English University Press, New York, pp. 107—118.

Hinrichs, J.R. (1966), *High Talented Personnel*, American Management Association, New York.

Hirch, I. *et al.* (1958), Increasing the productivity of scientists, *Harvard Business Review*, Vol. 36(2), pp. 66—76.

Horgan, N.J. and Floyd, R.P. Jr. (1971), An MBO approach to prevent technical obsolescence, *Personnel Journal*, Vol. 50(9).

House, J. (1969), Northern managers on the move, *Management*

Decision, Spring.

House, R.J. and Rizzo, J.R. (1971), American Psychological Association, Experimental Publication System, 12MS, p. 481, June, Washington DC.

Hughes, C.L. and Wass, D.L. (1970), Promoting goal seeking behaviour in managers, in Bass, B.M., Cooper, R. and Hass, J.A. (eds), *Managing for Accomplishment*, Heath, pp. 102—108.

Hughes, C.L. (1974), Help wanted: present employees please apply, *Personnel*, Vol. 51(4), pp. 36—45.

Institute of Electrical and Electronic Engineering, Transactions on Education (1976), Vol. 19(3), August, New York.

Immundo, L.V. (1974), Problems associated with managerial mobility, *Personnel Journal*, Vol. 53(12).

IPAT (1963), New prediction possibilities for vocational and educational counselling with the 16PF.

Jennings, E.E. (1967), *The Mobile Manager: A Study of the New Generation of Top Executives*, Appleton.

Johnston, R.H.W. (1976), *Continuing Education of Relevance to Engineers*, Institute of Engineers of Ireland, Dublin.

Jones, A.N. (1977), *Redundant Executives. An identification of their training needs and subsequent development of relevant training programmes*, The Industrial Training Authority, Dublin (unpublished).

Jones, A.N. (1979), *Managerial Obsolescence and Its Associated Factors*, Doctoral dissertation, UMIST.

Kahn, R.L., Wolfe, D.M., Quinn, R.P., Snoek, J.E. and Rosenthal, R.A. (1964), *Organisational Stress*, John Wiley.

Kaufman, H.G. (1974), *Obsolescence and Professional Career Development*, American Management Association, New York.

Kaufman, H.G. (1975), The older technical professional. Continuing education for up-dating technical people, *Research Management*, Vol. 18(4), pp. 20—23.

Knowles, M.S. (1970), *The Modern Practice of Adult Education*, Association Press, pp. 98—106.

Korchin, S.J. and Basowitz, H. (1957), Age differences and verbal learning, *Journal of Abnormal Social Psychology*, Vol. 54, pp. 64—69.

Kornhauser, W. (1962), *Scientists in Industry: Conflict and Accommodation*, University of California Press, p. 139.

Landis, F. (1969), Continuing engineering education — who really needs it? Paper presented at Continuing Engineering Studies, American Society for Engineering Education, Pittsburg, Pennsylvania, November 5th—7th.

Lawler, E.E. (1974), The individual organisation: problems and promise, *California Management Review*, Vol. 17(2), pp. 31—39.

Lazarus, R.S. (1966), *Psychological Stress and the Coping Process*, McGraw-Hill.

Lehman, H.C. (1963), *Age and Achievement*, Princeton University Press.

REFERENCES

Levene, M. (1976), *The Second Time Around*, Davis Poynter, London.

Locke, E.A. (1970), The supervisor as a motivator: his influence on goal setting, in Bass, B.M., Cooper, R. and Hass, J.A. (eds), *Managing for Accomplishment*, Heath, pp. 57—67.

McClelland, D.C. and Winters, D.G. (1969), *Motivating Economic Achievement*, Free Press, New York.

McGregor, D. (1960), *The Human Side of Enterprise*, McGraw-Hill.

McKinnon, D.W. (1962), The nature and nurture of creative talent, *American Psychologist*, Vol. 17, pp. 481—495.

Machlup, A. (1962), *The Production and Distribution of Knowledge in the United States*, Princeton University Press.

Mahler, W.R. (1975), Every company's problem — managerial obsolescence, *Personnel*, Vol. 42(4).

Mali, P. (1970), Measurement of obsolescence in engineering practitioners, *Continuing Education*, Vol. 3.

Mant, A. (1969), *The Experienced Manager*, BIM, London.

Marcson, S. (1960), *The Scientist in American Industry*, Harper & Row.

Margulies, N. and Raia, A.P. (1967), Scientists, engineers and technical obsolescence, *California Management Review*, Vol. 10(2), pp. 43—48.

Marn, F.C. and Heffernan, L.R. (1960), *Automation and the Worker*, Henry Holt.

Maslow, A. (1943), A theory of human motivation, *Psychological Review*, Vol. 50, pp. 370—396.

Meyer, H.E. (1974), *The Science of Telling Executives How They're Doing*, Fortune.

Miller, D.B. (1972), *Changing Job Requirements: A Stimulant for Technical Vitality*, American Society for Engineering Education, Continuing Engineering Studies Series, No. 7, pp. 133—146.

Miller, D.B. (1974), *Technical Vitality — Key to Extending Engineer's Productivity*, Paper presented at Workshop on Continuing Education for Engineers in Mid-Career, Dallas-Fort Worth, August 21st—22nd.

Minor, J.B. (1969), *Personnel Psychology*, Macmillan NY.

Minzberg, H. (1973), *The Nature of Managerial Work*, Harper and Row.

Morris, J. (1956), Job rotation, *Journal of Business*, October.

Morris, J. and Burgoyne, J. (1973), *Developing Resourceful Managers*, IPM, London.

Morris, J. (1975a), Developing resourceful managers, in Taylor, B. and Lippitt, G.L. (eds), *Management Development and Training Handbook*, McGraw-Hill.

Morris, J. (1975b), Managerial stress and the cross of relationships, in Gowler, D. and Legge, K. (eds), *Managerial Stress*, Gower Press.

National Advisory Commission on Health Manpower (1967), Vol. 1, November, US.

National Science Foundation (1969), *Continuing Education for R & D Careers*, Washington DC, NSF 69—20.

Norgren, P.H. (1965), *Pilot Study of Obsolescence of Scientific and Engineering Skills*, Columbia University.

Norgren, P.H. and Warner, A.W. (1966), *Obsolescence and Updating of Engineers' and Scientists' Skills*, Columbia University Seminar on Technology and Social Change.

Pedler, M., Burgoyne, J. and Boydell, T. (1978), *A Manager's Guide to Self-Development*, McGraw-Hill.

Pelz, D. and Andrews, F.M. (1966), *Scientists in Organisations*, John Wiley.

Penzer, W.N. (1973), Managers who don't grow up, *Management Review*, Vol. 62(1), pp. 2—16.

Perrucci, R. and Rothman, R.A. (1969), Obsolescence of knowledge and the professional career, in Perrucci, R. and Gerstl, J. (eds), *The Engineers and the Social System*, John Wiley.

Piaget, J. (1953), *The Origins of Intelligence in Children*, translated by Margaret Cook, International University Press Incorporated, New York.

Powell, L.S. (1969), *Communication and Learning*, Pitman.

Rand, T.M. (1977), Diagnosing the value rewards orientations of employees, *Personnel Journal*, Vol. 56(9), pp. 451—453.

Raudsepp, E. (1964a), Improving engineer productivity, *Machine Design*, Vol. 36(1), pp. 83—86.

Raudsepp, E. (1964b), Engineers talk about obsolescence, *Machine Design*, Vol. 36(15), pp. 148—151.

Reeser, C. (1977), Managerial obsolescence — an organisation dilemma, *Personnel Journal*, Vol. 56(1), pp. 27—31, 43.

Report on the Printing and Paper Industry (1977), Colin McIver Associates (Ireland) Ltd. for An Chomhairle Oiliuna (AnCO), Dublin.

Revans, R.W. (1971), *Developing Effective Managers: A New Approach to Business Education*, Longman.

Ritti, R.R. (1971a), Dual management. Does it work?, *Research Management*, Vol. 14(6), pp. 19—26.

Ritti, R.R. (1971b), Job enrichment and skill utilisation in engineering organisations, in Maher, J.R. (ed.), *New Perspectives in Job Enrichment*, Van Nostrand Reinhold, pp. 131—156.

Ritzer, G. and Trice, H.M. (1969), An empirical study of Howard Becker's side-bet theory, *Social Forces*, Vol. 47(4), pp. 475—478.

Roche, G.R. (1975), Compensation and the mobile executive, *Harvard Business Review*, November—December.

Roe, A. and Burach, R. (1967), Occupational changes in the adult years, *Personnel Administration*, Vol. 30(3), pp. 26—32.

Rogers, C. (1969), *Freedom to Learn*, Merrill.

Rogers, E.M. (1962), *Diffusion of Innovations*, Free Press of Glencoe, Illinois.

Rogers, J. (1970), *Using Broadcasts. A Guide for Tutors of Adult Groups*. BBC Publications.

Rogers, J. (1971), *Adult Learning*, Penguin.

Rosenbloom, R. (1967), in *Technology Transfer and Innovation*, National Science Foundation, Washington DC, NSF 67—5, pp. 107—109.

Rothman, R.A. and Perrucci, R. (1970), Organisation careers and professional expertise, *Administrative Science Quarterly*, Vol. 15(3), pp. 282–293.

Rothman, R.A. and Perrucci, R. (1971), Vulnerability to knowledge obsolescence among professionals, *The Sociological Quarterly*, Vol. 12(2).

Saunders, H.J. and Washington, C. and E.N. (1974), Continuing education: the intensified effort to keep up-to-date, *Chemical Engineering News*, May 13th, pp. 18–27.

Schein, E.H. (1967), Attitude change during management education: a study of organisation influence on student attitudes, *Administrative Science Quarterly*, Vol. 11, pp. 601–628.

Schein, E.H. (1968), The first job dilemma, *Psychology To-day*, Vol. 1, pp. 27–37.

Schultz, D. (1974), Managing the middle-aged manager, *Personnel*, Vol. 51(6).

Seidenberg, R. (1973), *Corporate Wives – Corporate Casualties*, American Management Association, New York.

Shumaker, C.H. (1963), Presenting the case for engineering and professional Societies. Paper presented at the Mid West Conference on Reducing Obsolescence of Engineering Skills, Illinois Institute of Technology, Chicago, March.

Siefert, W.W. (1964), The prevention and care of obsolescence in scientific and technical personnel, *Research Management*, Vol. 13(2), pp. 143–154.

Sleeper, R.D. (1975), Labour mobility over the life cycle, *British Journal of Industrial Relations*, Vol. xiii (2).

Smith, J.M. (1973), A quick measure of achievement motivation, *British Journal of Social and Clinical Psychology*, Vol. 12, pp. 137–143.

Sofer, C. (1970), *Men in Mid-Career*, Cambridge University Press.

Statistical Abstracts of the United States (1970).

Stein, M.I. (1968), Creativity, in Borgatta, E.F. and Lawler, W.W. (eds), *Handbook of Personality Theory and Research*, Rand McNally, pp. 900–942.

Stringer, R.A. (1966), Achievement motivation and management control, *Personnel Administration*, Vol. 29(6), pp. 3–16.

Tarnowieski, D. (1973), Middle managers, new values, *Personnel*, Vol. 509(1), pp. 47–53.

Tatsuoka, M.M. and Cattell, R.B. (1970), Linear equations for estimating a person's occupational adjustment based on information on occupational profiles, *British Journal of Educational Psychology*, Vol. 40(3), pp. 324–334.

Thompson, P., Dalton, G. and Kopelman, R. (1974), But what have you done for me lately? – The boss, *IEEE Spectrum*, Vol. 11, pp. 85–89.

Thompson, P.H. and Dalton, G.W. (1976). Are R & D organisations obsolete?, *Harvard Business Review*, Vol. 54(6), pp. 105–116.

Toffler, A. (1970), *Future Shock*, Bantam Books.

Van Atta, C.M., Decker, W.D. and Wilson, T. (1970), *Professional Personnel Policies and Practices of R & D Organisations*, University of California Lawrence Livemore Laboratories, Report 00735, pp. 1—71.

Vickers, D., Nettlebeck, T. and Wilson, R.J. (1972), Perceptual indices of performance: the measurement of 'inspection time' and 'noise' in the visual system, *Perception*, Vol. 1.

Vollmer, H.M. and McAuliffe, J.J. (1968), *Managerial Obsolescence*, a research report by the European Long Range Planning Service, Stanford Research Institute, US and Switzerland.

Walker, J.W. (1973) Individual career planning, *Business Horizons*, Vol. 16(1), pp. 65—72.

Waugh, N.C. and Norman, D.A. (1965), Primary memory, *Psychological Review*, Vol. 72(2), pp. 89—104.

Welford, A.T. (1958), *Ageing and Human Skill*, Oxford University Press for the Nuffield Foundation, Oxford.

Welford, A.T. (1962), On changes of performance with age, *The Lancet*, 17th February, pp. 335—339.

Welford, A.T. (1965), Performance, biological mechanisms and age: a theoretical sketch, in Welford, A.T. and Birren, J.E. (eds), *Behaviour, Ageing and the Nervous System*, Thomas.

Welford, A.T. (1968), *Fundamentals of Skill*, Methuen.

Welford, A.T. (1976), Psychomotor performance, in Birren, J.E. (ed.), *Handbook of the Psychology of Ageing*, Van Nostrand Reinhold.

Wheeler, E.A. (1968), Education for Anti-obsolescence? A survey of trends for engineers and scientists, *Training and Development Journal*, Vol. 22(6), pp. 21—26.

Wool, H. (1973), What's wrong with work in America? A review and essay, *Monthly Labour Review*, Vol. 96(3), pp. 38—44.

Zelikoff, S.B. (1969), On the obsolescence and retraining of engineering personnel, *Training and Development Journal*, Vol. 23(5).

Index